The Knowledge Corrupters

For Joan

The Knowledge Corrupters

Hidden Consequences of the
Financial Takeover of Public Life

Colin Crouch

polity

Copyright © Colin Crouch 2016

The right of Colin Crouch to be identified as Author of this Work has been asserted in accordance with the UK Copyright, Designs and Patents Act 1988.

First published in 2016 by Polity Press

Polity Press
65 Bridge Street
Cambridge CB2 1UR, UK

Polity Press
350 Main Street
Malden, MA 02148, USA

ISBN-13: 978-0-7456-6985-4
ISBN-13: 978-0-7456-6986-1 (pb)

A catalogue record for this book is available from the British Library.

Library of Congress Cataloging-in-Publication Data

Crouch, Colin, 1944-
   The knowledge corrupters : hidden consequences of the financial takeover of public life / Colin Crouch.
      pages   cm
   Includes bibliographical references and index.
   ISBN 978-0-7456-6985-4 (hardback) – ISBN 978-0-7456-6986-1
(pbk.)   1. Public-private sector cooperation.   2. Public administration.
   3. Human services.   4. Neoliberalism.   I. Title.
   HD3871.C78 2015
   306.3–dc23
                     2015011654

Typeset in 11 on 13 pt Sabon
by Toppan Best-set Premedia Limited
Printed and bound in the United Kingdom by CPI Group (UK) Ltd, Croydon

The publisher has used its best endeavours to ensure that the URLs for external websites referred to in this book are correct and active at the time of going to press. However, the publisher has no responsibility for the websites and can make no guarantee that a site will remain live or that the content is or will remain appropriate.

Every effort has been made to trace all copyright holders, but if any have been inadvertently overlooked the publisher will be pleased to include any necessary credits in any subsequent reprint or edition.

For further information on Polity, visit our website: politybooks.com

Contents

Abbreviations   vii
Acknowledgements   ix

1   Neoliberalism and the Problem of Knowledge   1

2   Knowledge and the Problem of Capitalism   32

3   The Corrosion of the Public-Service Ethos   66

4   Knowledge for Citizens, Customers or Objects?   97

5   Citizens, Customers, Politicians, Professionals
    and Moneymen   128

References   162
Index   171

Abbreviations

BBC	British Broadcasting Corporation
BMJ	*British Medical Journal*
BP	British Petroleum
CBI	Confederation of British Industry
CEO	chief executive officer
CQC	Care Quality Commission
ECB	European Central Bank
EU	European Union
FDA	Food and Drug Administration (US)
FSA	Financial Services Authority
GCSE	General Certificate of Secondary Education
GDA	guideline daily amount
GMO	genetically modified organism
HMI	Her Majesty's Inspectors (of Schools)
HMIC	Her Majesty's Inspectorate of Constabulary
HMRC	Her Majesty's Revenue and Customs
IMF	International Monetary Fund
IPPC	Independent Police Complaints Commission
LCP	Liverpool Care Pathway
MP	Member of Parliament
NHS	National Health Service
NPM	new public management

OECD	Organisation for Economic Co-operation and Development
Ofsted	Office for Standards in Education, Children's Services and Skills
PPI	payment protection insurance
RBS	Royal Bank of Scotland
TEPCO	Tokyo Electric Power Company
TUC	Trades Union Congress
UK	United Kingdom
US	United States
USCSHIB	United States Chemical Safety and Hazard Investigation Board

Acknowledgements

I could not have written this book without the collaboration of my wife, Joan. She gathered much of the material for it; enabled me to take advantage of her years of experience in administration of the English schools system for an understanding of the working of public service professionalism, inspection and similar issues; and helped me try to make my English more accessible to general readers.

I am also grateful for ideas and encouragement from my publishers, John Thompson of Polity Press and Heinrich Geiselberger of Suhrkamp Verlag (who pointed out to me the links between what I am trying to do and the US crime series *The Wire*).

As always, all remaining errors and infelicities are my own responsibility.

1

Neoliberalism and the Problem of Knowledge

In October 2014 it was revealed that the UK National Health Service (NHS) was offering medical practitioners £55 for every patient they diagnosed as suffering from dementia. Inadequate diagnosis of dementia had become a recognized problem in the country, and the idea was that doctors might be better motivated to identify cases if they had some money incentive to do so. There was a hostile reaction from many practitioners and patients groups. Over fifty practitioners wrote an open letter, published in the *British Medical Journal* (*BMJ* 2014), to the NHS leadership protesting that payments of that kind undermined the relationship of trust between doctor and patient, which was based on professional integrity rather than payment. Some patients groups were worried that doctors were being given an incentive to make exaggerated diagnoses of dementia. Many members of the wider public were puzzled to find the NHS using money payments in this way. They should not have been surprised. The idea that money is always the best motivator of human action, superior to reliance on professional competence, has been deeply embedded in the minds of decision-makers and managers in many walks of life for years now. Many of its implications have been far more damaging than a small financial incentive to make a dementia diagnosis. The purpose of this book is to explore some of these.

That as much of life as possible should be reduced to market exchanges, and therefore to money values, is one of the main messages of the most influential political and economic ideology of today's world, neoliberalism. It is in particular deeply embedded in the most dynamic and powerful sector of the world economy, financial services, where all values are expressed in terms of the prices that can be achieved by selling assets on to others who value them for the prices that can be achieved by selling them further on, in an infinite regress of prices based on nothing other than further prices. While this brings certain important advantages, such as clear criteria of comparison of one value against another, the idea that money is the best guide to value does considerable damage if unchecked. This problem is widely recognized, and much political debate today concerns certain major examples of it. For example, unrestrained economic activity harms the natural environment, but market forces themselves can do nothing about this. Values such as love and happiness cannot be expressed as market transactions without distorting their meaning. There is a wide consensus that inadequate access to money should not prevent people from enjoying basic rights to health, education, nourishment and housing. More strikingly, the use of the financial sector's approach in its own field brought the world to a major crisis in 2007–8. But a far less frequently noticed victim of the dominance of money as a guide to action is knowledge. It may seem surprising, as neoliberalism is itself a highly intellectual doctrine, rooted in theoretical knowledge. Also, many market economies are associated with strong scientific performance, which depends crucially on a knowledge base. My central claim that neoliberalism is an enemy of knowledge therefore requires considerable support – though the fact that distortions of knowledge clearly lay at the heart of the financial crisis makes my task of persuasion that much easier. In the pages that follow I shall provide support for my contention, and show the wider damage to human life, and in particular our attempts to ground it in ethical principles, that results from the knowledge-corrupting tendencies of neoliberalism, and why and how we must fight it.

My central claims are as follows:

1   The attempt to make public services behave as though they exist in markets – a fundamental neoliberal policy achievement – both brings to those services an over-simplification of the knowledge involved in them and undermines the professions that are the carriers of that knowledge. This is one of the issues involved in the dementia incentive payments case.

2   Although the market is itself a highly elaborate form of knowledge, heavy reliance on it undermines other forms, including the scientific knowledge that underpins much of modern life.

3   While early theories of the free market saw it as nested among actors who would act with moral integrity, the contemporary form of market theory as rational choice exalts and rewards dishonest behaviour that connives at the corruption of knowledge.

4   While pure market theory requires an economy with large numbers of producers and consumers, actual existing neoliberalism accepts high levels of concentration of monopoly power, the domination of sectors of the economy by very small numbers of large corporations. In certain cases this leads to powerful economic elites controlling access to and distorting knowledge to serve their own interests. In the following chapters I call this somewhat perverted, if dominant, form of neoliberalism, 'corporate neoliberalism'.

5   A final distortion concerns the knowledge we have of ourselves. To act fully effectively in the market involves being a self-centred, amoral calculating machine. When this is just one among a mass of

features of ourselves, this is not problematic. As the market and analogues of it spread into ever further areas of life, however, we have incentives to suppress these other features, and to know ourselves primarily as these machines.

The net result of these processes is that, as we move further into a world of markets that are unrestrained by either public regulation or a need to be trustworthy, and distorted by extreme concentrations of economic power, those of us outside the political and economic elite run high risks of being deceived. Many individual instances of this are widely perceived and resented, from the mis-selling of financial products by banks and insurance companies, to dishonest means of pursuing stories by newspapers, or to the rigging of performance scores by governments and public services. What needs to be demonstrated is that many of these disparate cases are all linked, and can be traced back to the exaggerated respect being paid to a rather contorted form of market economy. I obviously cannot claim that all corporate and political dishonesty can be blamed on the market, as corruption and deception exist in all types of economy, probably worst of all in state-controlled economies where there are no markets. But there are particular forms of these malpractices that do result from the way in which markets are currently being used, and they could be considerably reduced if contemporary policymakers took a less uncritical approach to markets and corporate power.

Democracy becomes a particular casualty, as accurate knowledge is its lifeblood. Where those exercising large quantities of power can obfuscate, confuse and corrupt popular knowledge, democracy becomes the prisoner of powerful interests. The issues debated in this book are therefore in part a continuation of themes that I launched in my *Post-Democracy* (Crouch 2004). But this observation raises a difficult challenge. In the following chapters I shall place considerable emphasis on the importance of professional knowledge, and the way in which it can be undermined by unchecked market forces and corporate power. In speaking of professionalism I am not pleading solely for the elite professions, but also for the wider realm of technicians, carers, and all others engaged in service delivery who need some discretion over the way they work and the quality they provide. But in either event, the relationship between that knowledge (which tends to be exclusive and held by an elite of practitioners) and democracy is problematic.

Advocates of both the market and the state will at times claim an alliance with professions; but both can also be antagonistic towards them, antagonism usually being expressed in the name of individual customer rights or democracy. For example, from time to time politicians insist that it is they whose relationship to the public is what is important in public-service delivery, and that professionals often operate as an arrogant and unresponsive elite. Advocates of the market will depict professionals, especially public-service ones, as imposing their own paternalistic judgement on what is in clients' best interests, when in a pure market they would be mere providers of what their customers want to have, customers being best able to judge their own interests. Many political arguments for setting markets against the power of professionals have been demotic appeals to liberate the population from the professionals' claims to superior knowledge – whether this refers to the knowledge of the welfare state professions or the scientists who warn us against such matters as global warming or the health risks associated with the products of junk food manufacturers. On the other hand, advocates of market forces in health services will sometimes argue that the market brings together health professionals and patients in an immediate relationship without interference from politicians and bureaucrats – though health professionals often oppose introducing financial exchanges into the high-trust relationship that they believe they need to have with their patients, as in the NHS dementia case. I shall return to these difficult issues in the final chapter. First, I need to support my contention that certain approaches to markets do damage to knowledge – and en route to trustworthiness and ethical behaviour.

In doing this I am in no way claiming that neoliberalism is the cause of current perceptions that trust is declining. I am not even claiming that there is an actual decline in either trust or trustworthiness; I rather share the view of Onora O'Neill (2002), in her excellent discussion of contemporary problems of trust, that we seem to believe that trust is declining rather than actually express less trust in our daily lives. Neoliberalism's role in all this is to claim that the market will resolve problems of trust by rendering it unnecessary. This is often true, as we shall see; but it is not always true, and there are certain ways in which the market can undermine trust.

Markets, Knowledge and Public Services

An example will show quickly what I mean by the first of my numbered points, and take us to the heart of the main issues at stake. It is not the best logical starting point; this would be point (2). But I have placed it first because it is the most politically salient and recognizable.

It has become fashionable since the 1980s to measure the performance of public services by setting targets for their practitioners – teachers, medical personnel, care services, police – their levels of success in achieving which are then converted into scores. These scores are publicized, sometimes to enable a service's users to choose among different producers, always to allow government leaders and service managers to behave like managers of private firms, rewarding those who maximize profits and punishing those who fail. The aim is to make choosing a public-service provider, or managing a number of service units, similar to dealing with shops or other market outlets, the performance scores playing the role of prices. According to market theory, and for simplicity staying with customers' rather than managers' perspectives, once customers have expressed certain initial preferences for taste and quality range, they choose goods on the basis of their comparative price: a single, simple indicator. That is the beauty of the market; it gives us in one datum all the knowledge we need to make effective choices. It is then argued that parents of schoolchildren, potential hospital patients and clients of old people's homes should be able to make similar simple comparisons. This, according to theory, will have two beneficial consequences. First, individuals will be able to make choices for themselves rather than have public authorities dictate to them. Second, all providers within a field will have an incentive to improve their performance according to the measured targets, or they will lose business – unlike in an old-style public service, where they could go on providing an unchallenged monopoly service to a captive population.

The gains that can come from this approach should not be discounted, particularly those from the second argument, which will also be of particular help to service managers. It is not so much the value of consumer choice as a thing in itself that is important as the incentive that the existence of choice gives to all producers to improve. However, the arrangement presents certain problems. Only a few elements of performance can be selected for inclusion in indicators, as a mass of data becomes too complex for users to apply. But this selection process has two negative consequences. First, someone has to choose the indicators, and this becomes government ministers and their officials and advisors. They can use indicators to direct attention to criteria that they want service users to apply, which are not necessarily those that users would have chosen from themselves. For example, as will be discussed in more detail in the following chapter, in the UK among the indicators that young people are encouraged by government to use when choosing which subject to read at university are the salaries typically achieved by graduates in various disciplines. The aim is to encourage young people to see education primarily in terms of its money value – rather than, say, the pursuit of intellectual curiosity or the pleasure of learning. It is reasonable for politicians to have such an aim, but to use half-concealed persuasion of this kind is not compatible with the rhetoric that accompanies the use of indicators of giving people a 'free' choice without interference from government. Rather, political interference is merely changing its style, using techniques of 'nudge' that are less openly authoritarian but by the same token less easy to discern and therefore to confront.

'Nudge' refers to the various techniques that firms, governments and others with the power to shape our environment use to encourage us to behave in ways that they want, without our realizing that they are doing it. The ways in which items will be located in a shop provide many examples. The transfer to the political field of such commercial techniques was pioneered by Thaler and Sunstein (2008). Sunstein was subsequently appointed to head President Obama's Office of Information and Regulatory Affairs, while the UK Conservative–Liberal Democrat coalition established a British Behavioural Insights Team (generally known as the 'Nudge Unit') within the Cabinet Office to explore the scope for using the ideas in British public policy. The point of nudge is to persuade people to act in ways that government wants without it having to regulate and control behaviour through legislation. Advocates of the political use of nudge draw attention to its role in health education, which was the main field in which Thaler and Sunstein were interested. One of their ideas was to explore how far the techniques used by food manufacturers to persuade people to eat unhealthy food could be used for exactly the opposite goal. This has been an entirely benign initiative. However, one can see how it can easily be used for less innocent and partisan purposes, persuading people to do things without their knowledge that this is happening to them.

A second problem with the indicator approach is that it entails placing overwhelming importance on a small number of, usually politically salient, elements of a service and relatively neglecting others, which is almost certain to be a distortion of the reality of service quality and its importance to users. This has a further distorting effect on workers in the services concerned, who are strongly encouraged to place all their efforts at strong performance on items covered by the indicators – at the expense of other aspects of their work. If governments have chosen exactly the right targets, and if the items left out from the measurement exercise are very clearly of inferior importance, this will be a valuable tactic; but often this will not be the case. To take another example from UK experience, considerable priority has been placed on medical practitioners seeing patients within a short period of their being referred for consultation, hospital waiting lists having become a political issue during the 1990s. Practitioners therefore have an incentive to prioritize giving patients their initial consultation over other elements of the health service to which they might allocate resources – such as preventive measures. There is an assumption here that the political judgement of politicians carries a democratic legitimacy that trumps what might be the alternative priorities of medical practitioners themselves, and possibly their patients.

This last point raises the profound issues of the relationship between electoral politics, democracy, professional judgements and people's preferences that I indicated will be a major preoccupation of the final chapter of this book. Can we always trust politicians to choose the most important elements? Is there a risk that they may give undue prominence to issues that have appeared in newspaper campaigns or other publicity-seeking activities? A particular problem here is that public services often deal with issues that are of considerable importance to our lives but where judgements about the best actions for us are very difficult. Advocates of markets may flatter us by saying that we are all competent to make these choices for ourselves, provided we are given a simple indicator analogous to a price. But should we expect to know exactly what aspects of a health service are most important for our well-being, when we are not medically trained? In any case governments are often using the indicator system to bias users towards certain choices for their own purposes, so the rhetoric about consumer sovereignty can be mendacious. Is there no source to which we can turn other than our own relative ignorance or the politically motivated indicators chosen by governments? Should we perhaps pay some attention to the people working in the services concerned, whose professional business it is to acquire a rounded knowledge of them and to devote themselves to high standards of performance? But can we trust them any more than we trust politicians? Neoliberal theory tells us that all human persons are primarily motivated by self-interest, that professionals systematically use their superior knowledge to trick us into rewarding them excessively and allowing them to behave as suits themselves rather than their clients, and that only the market is worthy of our trust, because only it has no human personality and therefore no interests. That is the mind-set that led to the UK NHS idea of offering medical practitioners money if they diagnosed a patient as suffering from dementia.

Knowledge and Markets

At this point an advocate of true markets will object that my examples do not concern real market services at all, but those that have been distorted by politics. In a real market schools, hospitals and other now-public services would be provided by private firms, just like any other product; no one would set targets, publicize league tables or issue guidance to customers (apart from commercial advertising). True believers in the market oppose even such devices as compulsory food labelling as political interference with consumer freedom. Provided there are many producers and many consumers, it is argued, the latter will work out their wants, and will express their preferences by choosing those products that best suit them. If there is, say, an overwhelming preference for short waiting times at hospitals, then hospitals that do not prioritize this will lose custom and will either change their practices to suit the demand or go out of business. On the other hand, if some customers for health services care about waiting times but others prioritize, say, ward cleanliness, then hospitals meeting alternative priorities will both thrive, attracting different parts of the population. Problems arise, it can be argued, when governments try to provide a halfway house between a state-determined service and a pure market one. From this argument emerges a highly important assertion, which lies at the heart of neoliberal theory and wrestling with which will play a major role in this book: *that the knowledge necessary for satisfactory choice lies in the market process itself, not in any human participant, whether provider, customer or government.*

The sum total of expressions of preferences through the market certainly provides a base of knowledge about our priorities that is beyond the reach of all elites, whether professional or political, who want to tell us what is good for us. The knowledge of these elites is always partial, in two senses of the word. First, it is always inadequate, because no one is all-knowing; second, the elites always have self-serving interests, and will interpret knowledge in ways that forward these. Teachers will tell us that class sizes should be small, as this increases the demand for teachers and therefore their salaries; the police will tell us that crime is becoming more complex, as this increases the demand for police personnel; politicians will tell us that they know what priorities a health service needs, as this enhances our respect for them and makes us more likely to vote for them. Only the market stands outside this confusion of inadequacy and self-seeking bias. The market gathers together all expressions of wants on the part of consumers, all claims to be able to meet those needs from producers, and matches these through the price mechanism in ways that avoid all human agency. The concentration of knowledge thereby achieved is greater than any human group can manage, and, provided markets are not dominated by small groups of producers or consumers, it is beyond the reach of human bias.

Therefore, although the use of targets and indicators in public services was part of a reform process designed to make such services more closely resemble goods in the market, from the perspective of thorough-going advocates of the market it is just an unsatisfactory compromise that causes more problems than it solves. Only a full privatization of these services, with customers buying their own education, health services, care, security and everything else, can give us the advantages of acting with the best possible knowledge that only the market can give. This raises many very familiar and much-debated issues about citizenship rights, collective goods, and inequalities in access to vital services resulting from differential ability to pay. Here our concern is limited to the issue of knowledge. What implications does this development in the argument have for my initial contention that knowledge is a victim of the spread of market processes? It would seem that the opposite is true, and that the market is knowledge's only reliable friend. To answer this question we need to explore further the thinking of market theorists who have asserted this claim on behalf of the market.

This task has been performed most expertly by Philip Mirowski (2013) in his study of neoliberal ideology. He singles out the writing of Friedrich von Hayek, the Austrian economic philosopher whose observations of both Nazism and Soviet communism in the middle years of the twentieth century led him to have a horror of state power and to advocate the maximal use of markets as a means of protecting human life from its grasp. He was no marginal figure, and it is reasonable to treat him, not just as a representative, but as *the* central figure in the articulation of neoliberal ideology. He was awarded the Nobel Prize for Economics in 1974. He founded the Mont Pèlerin Society, which has since the early 1950s been the main gathering point for economists and others, including many other economics Nobel Prize winners, hostile to state ownership of industries, government economic planning, the welfare state and other state interventions in the market economy. He was regarded by Margaret Thatcher as the main intellectual guide for her attempt to replace the social compromises of twentieth-century Britain with a more thorough-going neoliberalism. The influence of Hayek and his distinguished collaborators within what Mirowski calls the Neoliberal Thought Collective can be seen at many points in today's economic policy-making, from the general reduction in tax burdens on the wealthy to the deregulation of global finance.

It was Hayek (1944; 1948; 1960) who spelt out the idea of the market being a superior repository of wisdom, rendering all human attempts to second-guess it through the use of expertise imposed on its outcomes as necessarily inferior. At first sight, this seems in no way to be positing the market as the enemy of knowledge, but commending it as the only form that knowledge can reliably take – and a democratic, anti-elitist form at that. For example, neither medical experts nor patients can fully know which treatment is best for an individual patient; and over time the answer will change. However, if large numbers of patients can opt for particular treatments from a large number of practitioners within a fully marketized health service, a wisdom is gradually built up, emerging from the sheer mass of transactions. The knowledge generated in this way by the market is controlled by no one and belongs to no one; we all contribute to it, and we can all benefit from it. Pitting this kind of knowledge against that produced by organized bodies of experts is akin to pitting the theory of biological evolution against a creationist account of the origin of species – which is ironic, given that an important segment of believers in the free market in the US are creationists, while socialist sceptics about market forces are usually evolutionists. It is also ironic that neoliberals exalt the market as a public good, when much of their work is devoted to attacking the idea of public goods.

It should be noted that the Hayekian approach does not attack the idea of human knowledge as such, only attempts to use knowledge to make authoritative collective public policy decisions, to reach a kind of meta-knowledge. It does not say that there is no such thing as medical knowledge, or that medical practitioners have no better knowledge of what they are doing than a person with no medical training. Indeed, it is an approach that is in several respects friendly to science, because true science always accepts that current knowledge can be improved on, and that it is rarely possible to pronounce that a state of perfect knowledge has been reached. The constant minute adaptations possible in the market are better able to reflect this dynamic, changing nature of knowledge than attempts through organizational structures to pronounce on best practice. The approach is suspicious of attempts to draw conclusions on the basis of knowledge that then inform how systems of health provision are to be organized and priorities arranged within them. In particular it is suspicious of such attempts by governments or organizations of professionals. The former are suspected of wishing to impose a state socialist dictatorship; the latter of seeking to twist the provision of services to their own vested interests of a trade union kind.

Attractive though this is, the Hayekian theory has two major types of defect: defects in the way that the market itself operates, even when virtually pure; and those that result from the frequent practical impossibility of achieving such purity. The combined result of these defects is to turn the theory into a de facto enemy of knowledge (at least of widely distributed knowledge), a friend of powerful interests that seek to distort knowledge, and a further enemy of institutions that might confront the distorters.

Problems of the market for knowledge

We shall first examine certain problems of knowledge that the market cannot resolve even when it is working well; the second problem will be addressed when we turn to points (3) and (4) of my initial list. Economic theory assumes that participants in a market have perfect knowledge of their own wants and of the characteristics of the goods and services available for them to satisfy those wants. This does not mean that economists are unable to model markets of actors with imperfect knowledge; they routinely do this. But for the market to act as the repository of knowledge that the Hayekian theory requires, there must be no systematic inadequacies of this kind; inadequacies need to be adventitious, in which case they will cancel themselves out as market participants engage in a mass of transactions; that uncoordinated mass nature of its transactions is the feature that enables markets to accumulate all relevant knowledge. It is also assumed that the pure market itself gives its participants no incentives to ignore or, even worse, distort information available to them.

The problem with all this is that it is very difficult in real life for markets, except those for very simple standard products, to attain that degree of perfection. The more complex products become, the more difficult it is for markets to cope with the heavy demands that the theory places on them; and an important characteristic of life in modern advanced societies is that products do become ever more complex. We can take the highly important example of what are considered to be the most perfect markets of all, the financial markets, in the years leading up to the crisis of 2007–8. Until that time, critics of the application of market analogues to other fields of life tended to argue that the idea of maximizing on one indicator of success might work very well within financial markets; the problem lay in the transfer by inappropriate analogy to health, education, policing and so forth. But the crisis revealed the inadequacy of the approach in its own heartland.

The theory on which stock market trading is based is that of efficient markets. This holds that, if it can be assumed that investors are rationally motivated to discover all relevant information about a firm when risking their funds with it, it can also be assumed that the prices of a firm's financial assets, which reflect the outcome of these investors' assessments, tell us all that we need to know about the firm's performance. It is therefore not necessary for traders to acquire information about substantive performances themselves. All that matters is the price that assets can fetch in the market. This was a pure expression of the Hayekian model of market knowledge. It made it possible to develop the derivatives and secondary markets that produced extraordinary growth in the speed of share transactions and in stock values from the 1990s onwards. The prices at which stocks and bonds were traded became the sole guide needed to know what the assets covered by these prices were worth. Trader A simply needed grounds to believe that he could sell an asset to B, because B believed he could sell it to C, because C believed he could sell it to D... There was an expanding universe of financial trade, as markets became increasingly deregulated and as investors in the Far East and other parts of the world joined in the game. Accountancy practice changed in order to value firms at their current stock market valuations rather than, as had been done in the past, any attempt to calculate some 'real' value. The growth of these markets therefore seemed to reduce the need for information, other than the self-referential information being produced by the markets about themselves. Thus financial markets came to represent a higher reality than what people used to regard as the 'real' economy.

This is the process that triggered the financial collapse of 2007–8. Far from providing incentives to acquire information that would guarantee their perfect functioning, the financial markets gave participants a dangerous incentive to do the opposite. They came to believe that they could depend on one slender line of information – asset prices in futures trading – to tell them all they needed to know. Speed was of the essence, as perspectives were very short-term indeed. But asset prices had become heavily affected by a chain of guesses and gambles, and collapsed like a house of cards when these unravelled. Neoliberal economists have tried to argue that there was absolutely nothing wrong with their theories, and that had the US government not intervened in mortgage markets to encourage lending to poorer would-be house purchasers, everything would have rectified itself. That contention in itself can certainly be contested on factual grounds (Mirowski 2013: 301–23), but the point remains that expectations of asset trades in secondary markets became unreliable forms of information. The market did not convey perfect information; far from it. The financial crisis teaches us that the requirements made of the market if it is to replace all other knowledge are very stringent indeed; and that if they cannot be met, the consequences can be disastrous. It is therefore highly unlikely that the knowledge embodied in markets can replace other kinds of knowledge. If that is true of markets in their heartland, purely financial transactions, how much more important a lesson it is when markets are extended to other fields.

We must acknowledge that, given certain conditions, market participants' knowledge does not need to be perfect, but 'good enough' to enable them to make choices. For example, if I want to buy a car that minimizes atmospheric pollution, I do not need to understand the technology of pollution reduction in car engines and fuel types; it is enough that I have information about which vehicles produce the lowest emissions. If enough people like myself express such a preference in our market choices, some manufacturers will find it worth their while to produce vehicles with low emissions; the market will have generated knowledge about a desire for a reduction in vehicle pollution without the need for any governmental or expert action.

However, the 'certain conditions' necessary for my need for knowledge to be restricted in this way are important. There are at least two of them, and both provide problems for a system based purely on markets. First is a doubt whether the market, left by itself, would produce the knowledge that vehicle emissions are harmful, the knowledge that is necessary for consumers to have if they are to be concerned about emissions in the first place. Second is the trust in other knowledge sources that has to stand in for the inadequacies of our own direct knowledge.

To deal first with the former point, in practice the knowledge necessary to make decisions about vehicle emissions was discovered by scientists working in universities without any particular motivation to produce goods for the market. They were not entirely outside the market; they were motivated to make important discoveries by a desire to advance their careers within the academic labour market, and scientists working in systems that provide no such incentives might well not have bothered to carry out such research.

However, the fact that such research usually takes place in academic institutions, typically funded either by the state or by charitable funds, removed at one stage from engagement with commercial markets, serves as a warning that pure markets may be less efficient than other mechanisms at producing the knowledge that the market itself needs in order to function – but which some producers would sooner we did not have. Certainly, and following the analogy of biological evolution, we might expect that, given a market in which very large numbers of persons are trying to make a living by inventing new products, someone might hit on the idea of seeing if vehicle emissions damage the environment, and then trying to develop a market for selling that knowledge. But in practice that is not what happened. The chemistry of vehicle emissions is just one example among millions of where knowledge subsequently used in the market has been built up in the first place by a system of research organization that stands outside the market and is formed on largely (though not solely) different principles of operation. The market theory of knowledge is therefore at best an incomplete theory.

The weakness of market theory here is that it places all emphasis on the fact that, in a perfect market, the price mechanism concentrates all necessary knowledge into a single indicator, all partial pieces of substantive knowledge being amalgamated within it. We are here back with the example with which we began this chapter: the problematic role of indicators – whether in normal markets or their extensions by analogy into other fields – standing for a complex reality without those using them needing to have the substantive knowledge on which the indicators were based.

Market Incentives to Dishonesty

The second condition necessary for us to act in markets without complete personal knowledge takes us to my third numbered point at the outset of this chapter: the problem of honesty and trust. For me to use knowledge about vehicle emissions when choosing my car in the absence of my own detailed knowledge of the chemistry and technology requires me to trust that the available information about emission levels is accurate and truthful. In theory the market will make this possible if there is a large number of competing providers of knowledge about emissions, selling that information to potential purchasers of motor vehicles; these customers will of course prefer reliable providers of knowledge over sloppy or corrupt ones. This has the advantage that the knowledge providers need have no personal integrity themselves, as the market itself will weed out the dishonest, but there are three problems with this approach. First, decisions whether an information provider has been competent can only be made *post facto*, as by definition customers are unable to decide on the provider's competence before making a choice as to which provider to use; if they could make an informed choice, they would not need the provider's services. There may therefore be waste and cost before the *post facto* judgements can be made, but in the long run such problems should be ironed out. More serious is the waste that occurs if large numbers of customers all have to buy separate evaluations from the providers, in order to make a market. This happens, for example, in the UK when people need to buy a surveyor's report to test the quality of a house they are contemplating buying. Several potential purchasers might buy an evaluation of the same house, but each has to pay separately. More serious still, however, is the problem that if there is a genuine market in information with many suppliers, the choice of which one to trust becomes bewildering, and one begins to need an evaluation of evaluators. In practice this is usually solved by there being only a very small number of providers; but then there is no true market, and suspicions of market-rigging and informal collaboration are raised, bringing back ethical concerns.

The case of ratings agencies illustrates the two latter problems very well. These are active in the financial markets, evaluating the economic position of companies and even of national governments, to give investors some guidance other than prices. Ratings agencies solve the problem of wasteful multiple purchases of their services by having as their customers, not those seeking information, but the companies and governments being rated themselves. This raises the serious moral hazard that the agencies are serving the interests of those being evaluated rather than those wanting the information. The answer to that problem in market theory is that, in a free market, an agency that did so would clearly be seen to have offered excessively optimistic ratings, and would therefore lose reputation. However, if we turn to the dilemma of having a pure market with many providers and therefore confusion, or an oligopolistic market with imperfect competition, we find that this has been resolved in the direction of oligopoly. The ratings business is dominated by three firms: Moody's, Standard and Poor's, and Fitch's, all located in the same small district of Manhattan. Can such a situation function in the manner required for a market to guarantee the quality of information?

The answer to that question was again delivered in the economic crisis. All the banks and, later, national economies that experienced major problems had been very highly rated by all three ratings agencies. Several years later, all three have survived and flourished, without challenge from new entrants. The market model of information provision failed, but no negative consequences followed for those giving the poor advice, and no one in the financial world seems to care.

Worse than problems of this kind is the fact that the need to maximize profits in the market can lead participants into direct and blatant distortion of the indicators that others are using. Again, the events surrounding the financial crisis provide us with examples, which will be further discussed in the following chapter, of outright corruption and criminal dishonesty on a vast scale on behalf of some of the world's leading banks in, for example, the Libor and Forex scandals. These and similar corruption cases were resolved by legal intervention. For moderate neoliberals and German *Ordoliberalen* this kind of use of law is compatible with a need for external rules to maintain the market. These people accept the inadequacy of the market to solve all our problems of knowledge, and the value of regulators and others who try to gain knowledge of what market practitioners are doing. For purists, however, the market should be entirely self-monitoring; there should have been no regulation, and the problem should have been resolved by other firms avoiding trading in future with banks engaging in corrupt practices, giving them a market incentive to behave honestly. But in the absence of skilled and strong external monitoring, knowledge that corruption is going on could – and indeed did – take a long time to emerge, during which time a considerable amount of damage was done to those being cheated. Also, in theory there should have been reputational damage to the banks involved, if not to the entire financial system. However, those same banks are still flourishing, the world's financial markets still dominate the global economy, and bankers remain among the most highly rewarded persons on the planet. As with the earlier and wider problem of markets and scientific knowledge, the market creates knowledge very slowly and inefficiently. When its advocates ridicule problems of bureaucratic delays in regulatory systems or state and charitably funded research, they need to set against these the losses to efficiency incurred by leaving everything to the market. The fact that neither these cases nor the failure of the ratings agencies have led to major crises of confidence within the financial world suggests that all these questionable practices have been discounted by that world. Given that such a high proportion of major banks has been involved, they are unlikely to price themselves out of the market if they raise prices to customers to recoup the value of the fines they have had to pay for cheating those same customers. A few rounds of smart advertising can dispose of any reputational damage.

This leads us to consider the role of trust in reducing corruption and manipulation of knowledge in markets. Trust has more than one meaning. When I say 'I trust her', the most obvious, everyday construction that would be put on my remark is that I believe in the personal integrity of the person concerned, such that I am confident she would not act dishonestly even if there were no possibility of deception being discovered. But there is a second interpretation: I might mean that I am confident that, were she to act dishonestly, a system of surveillance and sanctions would discover the fact and punish her, the expectation that this would occur being so certain that she would not contemplate the dishonesty. In this second meaning I do not strictly speaking trust the individual herself, but the context of institutions within which she is acting. While the first meaning is the main use that we commonly make of the idea of trust among our personal contacts, the latter is the one that necessarily dominates impersonal exchanges, including those in the market. When a shopkeeper accepts the piece of plastic that you offer to pay for some goods, there is certainly some trust involved. But he does not need to trust you personally at all; you are often a complete stranger whom he will never again see. What he has to trust is the whole apparatus of the credit card company, its ability to detect forged cards, and its willingness to compensate shops that find themselves the subjects of credit card fraud. And he trusts this apparatus, not because he believes that the people who run the credit card company have excellent personal moral qualities, but because he believes that a company that did not secure its operations in this way would rapidly lose all customers. This is the kind of trust that the market can manage, most of the time very well.

There are, however, occasions when these mechanisms break down, as they depend on the availability of knowledge of what is going on in a context where the persons in charge of that knowledge have an incentive to distort or withhold it. Credit card companies probably stand no chance of concealing vulnerabilities to dishonesty in their systems. But the perpetrators of the various major financial frauds were able to conceal what they were doing for a damagingly long period of time. The longer the frauds continued without detection, the bolder they became. There would have been an overall gain to the efficiency and integrity of the system had the first, simple meaning of trust been available; if the people operating in these markets had been honest souls who just believed it would be wrong to cheat. However, unlike the second form of trust, which can be created by the market, this simpler form stands outside it. If such trust exists, then market actors could benefit from it, saving money on such monitoring as that done by ratings agencies, and being able to risk engaging in joint ventures with others without highly elaborate and expensive legal arrangements. However, while the market can benefit from personal honesty, it cannot create it; it is a positive externality.

Worse, the market can destroy personal integrity, to its own cost and to that of a wide range of other persons and institutions, as it gives us incentives to behave dishonestly. Moral inhibitions are, by definition, a deflection from profit-maximizing activity. A market trader who through personal scruple passes up the chance of a crooked deal which he can be highly confident will never be discovered is failing in his duty to perform his sole goal, to maximize profit. There is even an interesting economics literature on the 'problem' presented by senior managers who allow their personal moral scruples to make them pursue corporate social responsibility at the cost of reduced profits for their shareholders (see, for example, Jensen 2001). From the point of view of strict economic theory, moral inhibitions are no better than any other drag on the achievement of the highest level of efficiency. A truly rational market actor will not even have moral inhibitions about the need to obey the rules that entrench institutional trust, but will follow rules only if the cost of breaking them exceeds the gains to dishonesty. That is what rational choice means.

Not all theories of the market take this extreme position, though there has been a tendency for economists to move further towards it in recent times. For Adam Smith, the founder of classical economic theory, the market was embedded in taken-for-granted moral sentiments that led market participants towards honest dealing. However, according to the late twentieth-century theory of rational choice, which dominates thinking in both economic and political science, the only fully rational actor is one who subordinates all actions to the achievement of single maximizing goals. There is no place for moral sentiments.

It is a general assumption of sociological theory that no institution of governance can depend for its integrity on rules generated by itself, as the dominant actors within an institution can otherwise use those rules to corrupt it. All institutions need mechanisms from outside of themselves, beyond the reach of these actors. Thus political governance can be trusted only when it accepts the rule of law: that is, while being able to make laws, government must also be subject to them. Democracy is only secure when it is safeguarded by constitutional provisions that cannot easily be changed by those enjoying temporary majorities. Similarly, all except the smallest and most specialized markets need to be embedded in systems of external regulation, both to enable the monitoring of dishonesty and to maintain the level of competition that the market itself needs if it is to be a true market. These examples look to the formal institutions of law, but informal institutions such as interpersonal trust can also be relevant, guaranteeing the behaviour of powerful insiders, provided they are deeply embedded and rarely corrupted.

The Corporate Corruption of Markets and Knowledge

It has been entirely 'normal' during most of human history for minuscule elites to combine enormous holdings of wealth with political power, the gains made in each sphere strengthening those in the other. One among many aspects of that power has been the control of knowledge, through both subtle and highly crude means. The second half of the twentieth century saw a major change, though only within western Europe, North America and a small number of other parts of the world, in that government became democratic and inequalities of wealth and income declined considerably, though the very rich continued to exercise far more influence on public affairs than assumed in democratic theory. Since the 1980s that trend to reduced inequality has been reversed, first in the US and then in other democratic societies. The returns to wealth have been increasing faster than those to income from work done by the great majority of people, and within that, various mechanisms ensure that those with the very highest wealth have particularly high returns (Piketty 2013). This necessarily produces an intensification of inequalities. An increasing share of wealth and income are going to a small minority, often reckoned to mean the top 0.1 per cent or 0.01 per cent of the income distribution. The age-old process by which economic and political power are mutually convertible regains strength, but now in a context of formal political democracy. Government cannot be controlled as simply as in pre-democratic times. However, among the many things that the very rich can do with their wealth is to control knowledge in order to create climates of opinion favourable to their own interests. They can afford highly paid lobbyists; they can offer financial donations to politicians and can have access to them whenever they like; they might own newspapers and try to influence wider opinion; they can fund campaigns, mass organizations and even research institutes that produce evidence favourable to their cause and rubbish that of their opponents. They will use this influence to secure changes in regulation, government contracts and other favours that help them and their businesses become richer still. This in turn further strengthens their political power, and so on.

As with the problem of trust, theorists of the free market fall into two groups over this issue. There are those for whom heavy concentrations of capital and wealth are a threat to the competitive order, and need to be confronted through competition law. They would claim that only a true market economy could produce a healthy diversity of knowledge sources. There are, however, also those who see a competitive economy as meaning one in which competition creates winners, who then indefinitely receive extremely high rewards. These raise no objections to the use of inequality of wealth to try to influence public opinion. While both kinds of neoliberal can be found, the latter are considerably more vociferous. For example, although the Hayekian model of the market assumes a constantly maintained high level of competition and a mass of market participants, the Mont Pèlerin Society and other organs of Mirowski's Neoliberal Thought Collective, such as the World Economic Forum at Davos, almost never deplore the concentrations of wealth that are distorting the production and dissemination of knowledge. This is not surprising, as these groups have become the principal organs through which the very wealthy exercise their influence over knowledge. In this way too the market economy advocated by the principal articulators of neoliberalism has become a corrupter of knowledge.

Knowledge and the Restricted Self

I have mentioned changes in British higher education designed to encourage young people to see advanced study as a means to securing high salaries. In addition to the implications of this for the organization of universities (to be discussed in chapter 3), it also has consequences for how young people are being encouraged to see themselves. They should be instrumental calculating machines, not seeking pleasure or happiness through the possession of knowledge, but think-ing just of earnings opportunities. Mirowski takes this aspect of the growth of markets considerably further. If, as he argues is the contention of neoliberal thinkers, the market is the perfect store of knowledge, all aspects of life have to be converted into market form; otherwise they are being organ-ized inefficiently and are in danger of being left out of con-sideration. Starting with some insights into the idea of the fragmented self in market society of Michel Foucault (2004), Mirowski goes on to point out how human beings disappear into bundles of investments, marketable skills, temporary alliances, even perhaps tradable body parts. 'Freedom', in its popular meaning a cry from living, feeling human persons, becomes a set of disembodied, rationally selected opportunities. In the end we have no identity other than that which we derive from the market, as the market contains more knowledge about ourselves than we can acquire through any other means. In a striking passage Mirowski demonstrates the cynical meaninglessness of the idea of consumer sovereignty under such circumstances:

> When agents are endlessly desperate to refashion themselves into some imaginary entity they anticipate that others might want them to be, the supposed consumer sovereignty the market so assiduously pampers has begun to deliquesce. It is a mug's game to trumpet the virtues of a market that gives people what they want, if people are portrayed as desperate to transform themselves into the type of person who wants what the market provides. (Mirowski 2013: 115)

For all the professed concern of neoliberals with liberation of 'the individual', the individual self that is at the heart of their theories is not a human self in the sense we normally understand it at all. In their attempt to turn us into a new type of person, with a distinctive knowledge of who we are, neoliberals have ended up being like the totalitarian ideologists of fascism and communism to whom they imagine themselves to be the perfect antithesis. This extraordinary reversal has taken place in the following way. First, the superior efficiency of the market as the key processor of knowledge is established. Second, it follows that if areas of life not normally constituted as part of the market remain outside it, they will be neglected. Third, therefore, if such neglect is to be avoided, these other areas of life need to be redefined so that they have no characteristics other than those that can be covered by market calculation. If this project were to be completely successful, we should be unable to conceive of ourselves except as self-interested calculating machines.

Important pioneering work on this theme has been done by Gary Becker, another member of the Mont Pèlerin group.

In his economic theory of the family (1960) he demonstrated how a process of 'assortative mating' led 'high-quality' (i.e. wealthy) persons to seek out similar ones as marital partners, and analysed the supply of and demand for children in terms of their relationship to those for other goods on which a couple might spend money. He also developed the idea of labour as 'human capital' (1964), a resource divorced from the persons providing it. As contributions to economic theory these have been penetrating, and they have been useful in empirical analyses of behaviour. The problem comes when corporations, governments and other power centres, whether by the use of authority or by subtle 'nudge', seek to stress these conceptions of the human self at the expense of others, as in the British university application case. Other examples include: policymakers interpreting a growth in motherhood among teenagers without partners as a problem of excessive payments of maternity benefits; the encouragement of people on low incomes and students to take on various kinds of debt that they might not be able to afford, in order to bring them into the world of finance; and the relaxation of controls on gambling, in order to encourage people on low incomes to think of many aspects of their lives in terms of odds related to financial gain.

Unlike totalitarianism, neoliberalism is rarely in a position to impose on us its view of how we should perceive ourselves; we can always reject the attempted exclusion of emotions and values from our knowledge of who we are. That is why liberal capitalist societies are immeasurably more acceptable places in which to live than fascist or state socialist ones. However, the more areas of social life that are exposed to market calculation, the more difficult it becomes to hold on to those other forms of knowledge, and the more we drift towards being what Herbert Marcuse (1964) called 'one-dimensional man'. Marcuse was writing before gender consciousness had developed to its present proportions. However, the fact that, on the whole, the characters of women's lives expose them to a wider range of forms of knowledge of what constitutes human life than the more economy-bound male gender might make his unconsciously gendered concept more acceptable than it at first seems.

Plan of the Book

These themes will be pursued in the following chapters by exploring the fate of knowledge and its relationship to key participants in the main relevant economic contexts.

First, in chapter 2, we shall address knowledge and the private sector. Here we shall explore tensions between profit maximization on the one hand and professional knowledge and/or service quality on the other. In general, service quality is necessary to competitive success, but there are important situations in which competition on quality is overtly sacrificed to that on price. This might be considered to be a matter of reasonable market choice, but where activities are totally dependent on high-quality (and expensive) professional knowledge, that choice becomes questionable – particularly where it is a matter of the knowledge available to consumers. While nearly all the political debate about relations between the professions and consumers has concerned public services, some major issues also arise in relation to complex private products, such as food and medicine. A separate issue concerns the role of firms whose business it is directly to own and control flows of information.

In chapter 3 we shall see how these issues change where services are in the public sector. Arcane knowledge is one reason why some services have been located primarily in that sector: inadequacy of knowledge necessary to make customer decisions is a form of market failure. In the public sector the consumer sometimes loses the ability to choose between levels of quality of service, but gains absence of profit motive. In general, in public services the role and power of the professional service provider loom larger, creating some serious problems, which neoliberal theory has tried to address in various ways.

Debates over the contracting out of public services bring the relationship between professional and public in a market context to particular prominence. This will be the subject of chapter 4. Governments seeking both to contract out and to reduce costs can undermine the position of professionals, and this has implications for the treatment of the knowledge of those professionals. Issues emerging from this include the problem of communication of knowledge, and the position of trust and who deserves it among politicians, private-service owners and managers, and professionals.

Finally, chapter 5 will try to articulate new forms of relationship between citizens, professionals and others more compatible with democracy than those to which we are moving.

I have not had the resources to conduct a thorough research exercise, in which I would have searched exhaustively for as many cases as possible of the problems discussed, across a wide range of countries. I have been limited to examples that came my way as they might also have done to many other reasonably alert citizens. One negative consequence of this approach is that British examples loom particularly large, as that is the country to which I belong. However, since the UK has moved further along the neoliberal paths described here than many other, particularly western European, countries, it is likely that this nation does provide a high proportion of relevant instances. A second negative consequence is that I cannot claim to be testing strong hypotheses. For example, I cannot argue that the takeover of childcare in the UK by private equity firms has led to more cases of child abuse than had services been left in the hands of public-service professionals, as my evidence provides no basis for such a claim. I can only make smaller, mainly negative claims. For example, my evidence on childcare does demonstrate that privatization of this kind has not solved any problems in childcare; otherwise I would have been able to find no cases of malfunctioning under private ownership. Similarly, I cannot claim that the growth of performance targets and league tables in the public-service professions has produced a degree of distortion of professional behaviour that would not otherwise have existed, as we do not know what malpractices might have developed in the absence of targets. But I can show that these performance regimes have produced their own distinctive forms of distortion, and have certainly not resolved problems of trust in relations between professionals and their clients.

2

Knowledge and the Problem of Capitalism

When British Petroleum (BP) developed its oil exploration activities in the Gulf of Mexico, its engineers knew that certain margins of safety were required for the operations, and repeatedly warned senior managers that these were being risked. But financial knowledge taught that responding to these concerns would be highly expensive and would threaten the corporation's profit margins. In April 2010 BP's Deepwater Horizon rig exploded, killing eleven men and polluting a vast area of the Gulf in the US's worst ever environmental disaster. The spill continued for 87 days, killing large quantities of marine wildlife, ruining the livelihoods of thousands of people, and eventually costing BP at least $43 billion in fines and damages, as well as extensive harm to its reputation. In September 2014 a US District Court ruled that BP had been 'reckless' as well as 'negligent', which could increase legal claims against it by a further $18 billion, though at the time of writing the firm is appealing against this. Financial knowledge acted like an auto-immune disorder, trumping engineering and geological knowledge within the firm, eventually at vast cost to BP's finance-driven profit maximization strategy itself.

On 11 March 2011 an enormous earthquake and consequent tsunami struck the eastern coast of Japan. Among the mass of disasters unleashed by these events was serious damage to the Fukushima nuclear power plant, with leakages of nuclear material and considerable danger to the staff engaged in trying to repair the reactors. The official report into the incident stated in its opening paragraph that, although the initial disasters were natural, 'the subsequent accident at [Fukushima]...was a profoundly manmade disaster – that should have been foreseen and prevented' (National Diet of Japan 2012). The report argued that:

> [the] accident was the result of collusion between the government, the regulators and TEPCO [Tokyo Electric Power Company], and the lack of governance by said parties. They effectively betrayed the nation's right to be safe from nuclear accidents...We believe that the root causes were the organizational and regulatory systems that supported faulty rationales for decisions and actions, rather than issues relating to the competency of any specific individual. (National Diet of Japan 2012: 16)

The commission blamed what it regarded as specific aspects of Japanese culture for these failures, in particular excessive respect for hierarchy and organizational practices. But the outcome looks remarkably similar to what happened in the Anglophone culture of BP in the Gulf of Mexico: a suppression of knowledge about geology, engineering and the requirements of safety because these had very expensive implications, clashing with financial knowledge about the level of safety costs that would be compatible with making a profit.

The labels of 'learning society' and 'knowledge society' are today often proposed either as descriptions of an existing reality or as an aspiration. But, as the BP and TEPCO cases show, some of the behavioural incentives provided by contemporary economic organization threaten the use that we make of knowledge. The problem lies in the combination of the desire to use knowledge to maximize rational efficiency with the idea that the shareholder-value-maximizing capitalist enterprise forms the best vehicle for that task. Financial expertise has become the privileged form of knowledge, trumping other kinds, because it is embedded in the operation of banks, accountancy firms, hedge funds, the owners of private equity and other financial institutions – the institutions that ensure profit maximization. Under certain conditions this dominance of financial knowledge can become self-destructive, destroying other forms of knowledge on which its own future depends – just as an auto-immune disorder of an organism involves its immune system attacking characteristics of the organism on which its health depends.

We should not conclude from disasters of the Gulf of Mexico and Fukushima kind that whenever financial expertise suggests one course of action and another body of knowledge another, the former will always be wrong. There will be many cases where financial judgement leads to the avoidance of waste and of the inefficient use of resources. But it is important that we understand the various circumstances under which these conflicts can occur, as we need to be alert to the possibilities that the dominance of finance is crushing the intimations and warnings of other forms of knowledge.

We can identify at least five forms that this conflict can take. First, as in the BP and TEPCO cases, there can be a straight conflict between the paths indicated by financial and some other form of expertise. Second, the profit motive may lead firms to try to withhold information from customers that would be to the latter's advantage. Third, and more sinister, the dictates of profit maximization can give market actors incentives to distort and corrupt knowledge, either of a financial or some other kind. Fourth, firms may seek to control the generation as well as the dissemination of knowledge, so that it follows their profit-making incentives rather than wider goals. For example, they might do this by putting pressure on governments to favour certain kinds of research, or more directly when they themselves fund research. Finally, often leading on from this last, firms may seek to acquire ownership over certain forms of knowledge, removing it from its status as a public good. We shall discuss each of these possibilities in turn.

The Conflict between Financial and Other Expertise

Different kinds of knowledge might often give us conflicting advice as to how we should act. To take a homely example, we might know that, to achieve a certain body weight and figure, we should avoid certain foods; but that same diet might imply nutritional deficiencies. In such cases we either allow one kind of knowledge to trump the other, or we seek a compromise between them. Such dilemmas are normal. Serious problems arise when one kind of knowledge systematically triumphs over others, leading to serious distortions in our actions. This is threatening to happen in the fields of both corporate and governmental behaviour, as financial knowledge comes to dominate all others. In business this results from changes that have taken place in corporate governance, which make maximizing the share price the primary, even the sole, goal of managements. Contemporary accounting practice values firms solely in terms of their stock market performance, which responds to profit levels (or indeed, mere rumours about profit levels). It does not make assessments of a firm's longer-term viability, unless this happens to be expressed in share prices. A firm that under-performs in these terms is vulnerable to takeover. A similar situation affects governments following their increasing dependence on a small number of large, global banks for funding, with a consequent need to place the financial priorities of these banks at the heart of their own actions.

In the corporate sector it is by no means unknown for traders to spread false knowledge or exaggerated rumours about a firm's weaknesses in order to profit from a decline in share values. In a process known as shorting, the trader borrows to acquire a firm's stocks. The false knowledge is then disseminated; the price falls; at a certain point the trader buys back the stock at the lower price, making a profit. The extraordinary profits available in today's financial markets can give investors incentives to distort knowledge.

We can see how these situations occur through a series of examples.

First, we can return to the BP and TEPCO cases. They were both extreme instances, and the BP case might be regarded as untypical of modern corporate conduct; but it was untypical not just because of the size of the disaster, but also because BP is a corporation that makes exceptionally strong claims to its acceptance of corporate social responsibility and its sensitivity to environmental safety. It is in many respects a model corporation. The Gulf disaster can therefore in no way be written off as the freakish behaviour of a rogue firm. Further, one of its main partners in the Gulf, Halliburton, one of the world's largest oil services firms, was also no marginal outsider. It was closely associated with a former US vice-president, Richard Cheney, and had major contracts with the US government during the Iraq war. This connection may, however, be an inadequate guarantee of good behaviour. Cheney had been a prime mover in the Iraq war, and Halliburton has been found guilty in the US courts of corruption in its handling of the Iraq contracts. Further, in July 2013 Halliburton, which had been claiming that BP was responsible for any misdeeds at Deepwater Horizon, pleaded guilty in a US court to destroying evidence wanted by BP to make its own case. Nevertheless, Halliburton remains a prominent firm at the heart of the US economy; if it is indeed a 'rogue' firm, it is a respected insider rogue.

Despite its own good image and reputation, BP had already been dogged by safety problems. In 2005, 15 workers had died and 170 been injured in an explosion at a BP plant in Texas City, Texas. Subsequent investigation by the US Chemical Safety and Hazard Investigation Board (USCSHIB) cited corporate cost-cutting and a failure to invest in safety and accident prevention as among the causes (USCSHIB 2005). Heavy fines were imposed, and these were increased in 2009 when it was discovered that BP had failed to implement recommended safety improvements. Following the Gulf disaster, BP sold the Texas plant. Nonetheless, there had been signs that the corporation had decided to place more emphasis on safety. A new chief executive, Tony Hayward, was appointed and pledged to clean up the poor safety record associated with the reign of his predecessor, Lord Browne – not that Browne had been accused of any personal complicity in that record. However, the *New York Times* (Urbina 2010b) reported on 29 May 2010 that BP scientists had expressed concerns about the safety of Deepwater Horizon in June 2009. US Congressional hearings in May 2010 learned that BP and its two US associates, Halliburton and Transocean, had all ignored the results of tests in the weeks before the explosion that had revealed faults in safety equipment and the concrete around the rig. In October 2010 President Obama's investigator into the disaster found that 75 per cent of laboratory safety tests carried out for BP and Halliburton on the concrete in Deepwater Horizon had failed; but the firms had continued using the concrete (Broder 2010). Even after the Deepwater Horizon disaster the oil firms tried with some success to overturn the Obama administration's attempt to impose a moratorium on continued drilling in the Gulf while inquiries into the disaster were completed (Calkins 2011).

Deepwater Horizon was exceptional for the extraordinary size of the damage it produced. It also happened in the US. For these reasons it attracted enormous attention and scrutiny. (In December 2010 WikiLeaks (Webb 2010) leaked a report from the US ambassador in Azerbaijan that a disaster not unlike Deepwater Horizon had occurred 18 months earlier at a BP site there; but events in that part of the world are not widely reported.)

As I have suggested, this private corporate behaviour spreads to government agencies when these too are obsessed with providing profitable environments for business. The BP case demonstrates this too. The *New York Times* reported in May 2010 (Urbina 2010a) that the National Oceanic and Atmospheric Administration had been expressing concern since September 2009 that officials at another agency, the US Minerals Mining Service, had been over-ruling warnings from its own scientists about the environmental impact of oil extraction activities in the Gulf. On some occasions the scientists had even been required by senior management to change their reports. The Fukushima case also revealed complicity between the corporation and regulatory agencies, the Diet of Japan's report talking explicitly of regulatory capture. It argued that the Nuclear and Industrial Safety Agency had knowledge that the nuclear plant needed structural reinforcement to conform to new guidelines on resisting earthquakes, but had allowed TEPCO to address the issues at its own speed.

As a result of the prominence of these two incidents we came to learn far more than usual about corporate practices. We clearly cannot conclude from them that all major corporations allow the pursuit of profit to lead to scientific knowledge being ignored, but we are made aware of the strength of the incentives to do this. What saves us from more disasters of this kind is that managers often have the choice of judging that the short-term profit that might come from ignoring safety will be overwhelmed by financial and reputational losses. The unaided market itself cannot be relied upon to ensure that the best-informed decisions will always be taken, without such human intervention. However, modern Anglo-American corporate governance principles accept no legitimate interests in a corporation other than those of shareholders, which are identified with profit maximization. The role of senior managers is to be solely the agents of their principals, the shareholders, ensuring that the profit-maximization goal is achieved. The ideal shareholders in the model are not individual long-term holders of a company's shares, but units of action that buy and sell rapidly according to market signals; the perfect form of such shareholders is not human beings at all, but the computers that automatically buy and sell stocks in response to small movements in prices. This is a perfect practical expression of the

Hayekian ideal outlined in the previous chapter: all relevant knowledge is held in market prices; human intervention, with its prejudices and fallibility, cannot interfere. If such an approach comes to dominate completely, nothing could stop disasters such as the Gulf of Mexico or Fukushima from occurring.

However, as neoliberals will rightly remind us, these incidents give us little grounds for confidence that Hayek's bête noire, the regulatory state, will protect a wider public interest. As both cases showed, public bodies can be very responsive to corporate priorities. This is an aspect to which we shall return.

Similar issues apply in the relationship between financial expertise and scientific and other forms of innovation within companies. It is frequently alleged that the short-term pursuit of financial goals for which current corporate governance gives such strong incentives inhibits firms from pursuing innovation that might be costly but which, in the long term, might deliver more profit. In September 2009 the Aspen Institute in Colorado organized a meeting on this theme, attended by various corporate leaders and figures from government and academia. Their report began with a declaration:

> We believe a healthy society requires healthy and responsible companies that effectively pursue long-term goals. Yet in recent years, boards, managers, shareholders with varying agendas, and regulators, all, to one degree or another, have allowed short-term considerations to overwhelm the desirable long-term growth and sustainable profit objectives of the corporation. We believe that short-term objectives have eroded faith in corporations continuing to be the foundation of the American free enterprise system, which has been, in turn, the foundation of our economy. Restoring that faith critically requires restoring a long-term focus for boards, managers, and most particularly, shareholders – if not voluntarily, then by appropriate regulation. (Aspen Institute 2009)

It can hardly be maintained that the US economy has a low level of innovation, though it is also the case that, given its wealth, it tends to perform less well than those of northwest European nations that are less committed to the shareholder-maximization model of corporate governance (Crouch 2015: 236). There will always be room in the market for firms that seek niches as strong innovators, and attract either shareholders or committed venture capitalists who understand and appreciate that. It is certainly not possible to argue that capitalist economies are particularly incompetent at encouraging innovation, given their superior record to other kinds of economic system. The conclusion that we can, however, legitimately draw is that the market does not guarantee an appropriate balance between short-term financial goals and longer-term ones. This is because, almost by definition, it is not possible to quantify the gains that will flow from an innovation that has not yet been made, while short-term share market gains can always be predicted. The more corporate conduct shifts towards the latter, as has been the pressure of all corporate governance changes in recent years, the more the balance will be skewed in this direction. Contrary to neoliberal beliefs, the financial markets can get things wrong, whether it is a matter of safety and environmental damage, or the discouragement of long-term innovation. We cannot rely on the market to solve our problems of assessing the relative importance of different kinds of knowledge (Erturk et al. 2004).

Further kinds of problem that result from the dominance of financial expertise over all others were made evident by the financial crisis. In the previous chapter we briefly considered the role of ratings agencies and the failure of the attempt to use them as a kind of knowledge that is more substantive than that of the market but produced according to market analogues. A further aspect has been the attempts to resolve the debt crisis of some southern European countries by the imposition of austerity and deregulation alone. This can be seen particularly clearly in the case of Greece, which had to apply to the EU, the European Central Bank

(ECB) and the International Monetary Fund (IMF) (in combination, the so-called 'Troika') for massive support. The terms on which help was offered were set down clearly in a formal document (Government of Greece 2012). The country had to impose massive cuts on public spending, including public-service wages, to dismantle most labour market regulation and protection, and to reduce the role of collective bargaining (and therefore of trade unions) in setting minimum wages. The main aims of the labour market sections of the conditions were to expose workers to the full force of global labour market competition, requiring that country to compete on low prices alone; forget about the importance of up-skilling and improving the quality of the labour force that had hitherto been the main message of EU labour policies. The only interest shown by the Troika in infrastructural issues such as transport and energy was to ensure privatization and therefore profit-making opportunities for other European corporations. The document showed no interest in upgrading either human or physical infrastructure as such. The same approach was also applied, though less roughly, to other countries in difficulties: Ireland, Italy, Portugal and Spain.

The major concern of the Troika was to satisfy the private banks that had loaned money, and the German Bundesbank. Indeed, a committee of the main banks involved in having lent money to Greece was an informal but centrally important participant in the Troika's discussions. The banks were interested solely in getting back the money they had lent Greece – money lent on the basis of purely market knowledge about their capacity to sell the debt on, with little substantive knowledge about the potentiality of the Greek economy. Now they had no concern for what might happen to the Greek and other economies involved in the longer run. The Bundesbank has as a fundamental belief that only financial instruments are relevant to public policy-making. Therefore, no one with influence was concerned to ask substantive questions about the kinds of economic and other structures that might enable or require the debtor countries to upgrade their economies. Knowledge of this kind certainly exists, in accumulated research evidence of the infrastructures, kinds of public spending, skills and labour regime associated with the most successful advanced economies. True, this knowledge does not give unambiguous answers; but that means that it can provide a range of options. In the event only knowledge drawn from the world of finance was permitted, everything else being ignored. Countries are therefore being required to improve their performance in a context of falling demand (and therefore reduced activity) and deteriorating infrastructure.

The Incentive to Withhold Information from Customers

Firms must be expected to try to maximize their profits by any means possible. In principle this can include deceiving customers as to the nature of their products, but in economic theory customers are protected against such behaviour by competition: a firm that sells harmful or misleadingly described products will soon lose business; only honest producers will survive. That is how the market guarantees honest outcomes without producers themselves needing to be honest persons, and how it protects us from the dishonesty that it takes for granted will exist. For extreme neoliberals, this is the only protection that consumers need or on which they can rely, and these neoliberals will therefore be found opposing consumer protection laws. The problems of consumers of complex products not being able fully to understand the characteristics of the goods they buy makes it difficult for neoliberals to make this argument very directly; instead, they usually attack consumer protection as excessive bureaucracy. A few examples of over-zealous officialdom enable whole areas of protection to be ridiculed, as has happened to health and safety legislation. But this does not work in the face of serious problems of consumers' need for accurate information. We see neoliberalism in action in corporate campaigns to ensure that information is withheld from customers. The fact that such campaigns often fail, and that today's consumers receive considerable protection, testifies to the continuing strength of democracy, but it does not weaken the fact that the attempts take place, and that extensive resources are devoted to them. The issue of consumer information is not resolved within the market at all, but within the political arena, where campaigners for consumers confront the resources of corporate lobbying.

A major example of this conflict, where corporations were successful in reducing information available to consumers, was the European debate in 2010 over food labelling. Policymakers in most European countries had become convinced that action needed to be taken to inform consumers of the nutritional values of ingredients in the food they purchased, especially where potentially harmful substances such as fats and salts were concerned. Consumer groups and various medical and nutritional professional bodies favoured a 'traffic light' scheme, developed originally by the UK Food Standards Agency. Numbers indicating the proportion of a guideline daily amount (GDA) of particular ingredients represented by a given quantity of the food would be prominently displayed on the front of food packages, inserted in green, amber and red circles indicating the health quality of the ingredients concerned. Major food-producing corporations favoured instead a system listing the GDAs in small type in simple black and white, and not necessarily on the front of packaging. Research had shown that customers preferred the traffic light approach, and several major retail (but not food-producing) groups decided to adopt it voluntarily. Nevertheless, a group of leading food manufacturers lobbied the European Parliament very heavily, and in June 2010 the Parliament voted to support the manufacturers' line and oppose the traffic light scheme. It did, however, decide that the GDA list should be presented on the front of packages. In December the Council of Ministers of European countries also agreed not to adopt the traffic light system – but went further than the Parliament in accepting the food industry lobby's demands: the final EU-wide legislation did not insist that the GDA information should be placed on the front. In September of the same year the UK government stripped its Food Standards Agency, the 'traffic light' pioneers, of responsibility for nutritional labelling. The agency was at that time also stripped of many other powers, the UK government believing that the regulation of food quality was best left to the market.

When food (and other) manufacturers want to draw attention to a characteristic of their products, they use bright colours and large lettering, and place their boasts and claims prominently on the front of packages. They would never position their boasts in small black-and-white lettering on the back of a packet. For them to campaign for nutritional information to have the latter rather than the former characteristics can mean only a desire to reduce consumers' access to the knowledge concerned. Very large sums are spent by the food and alcohol industry on campaigns to prevent governments from requiring it to present health information to consumers (Miller and Harkins 2010).

The market sometimes works to force consumer information from firms. The UK-based food giant Tesco had originally joined with food manufacturers in opposing the 'traffic light' system. However, following adoption of it by most other major UK food retailers who maintain their own brands, by August 2012 Tesco had changed its line. But in the face of monopolistic positions by many large food manufacturers, and of heavy and successful lobbying of governments and parliaments, *both* market competition *and* political regulation are often proving inadequate to safeguard consumers' interests. This is happening at a time when product contents are increasingly complex and difficult for an ordinary consumer to discover.

The Incentive to Distort and Corrupt Knowledge

So far we have considered only attempts to withhold accurate information from customers. Considerably more sinister are the financial incentives given to firms to distort knowledge. Again, often these attempts are eventually found out, sometimes to the cost of the profit-making goal itself – the disease of the economy's auto-immune system again. More accurately perhaps, some of these attempts failed, and so we have knowledge of them; we do not know how many continue undiscovered. The point is that, were we to succumb to the neoliberal argument and allow only the market to find out what has been happening, we should discover far less.

The most disturbing examples of this phenomenon have emerged from the major scandals affecting some of the world's leading banks, laid bare following the financial crisis. Among them have been the Libor and Euribor scandals. Libor is the London InterBank Offered Rate, Euribor the equivalent operating in the Eurozone. Both are based in London. The Offered Rates are interest rates derived daily by the banks from information that they submit on their perception of how various interest rates are moving. Libor and Euribor affect very large numbers of future interest rates throughout the world, but they are entirely unregulated and assume total trustworthiness and honesty among banks to report rates without regard to how these might affect their own interests. This is a leftover from the days when the slogan of the London Stock Exchange was 'My word is my bond.' During 2010 it became clear that some banks were rigging the Libor and Euribor rates by misreporting their evidence in ways that would earn them very large sums of money, at the expense of other participants in the market. The first to be tracked down was Barclays, one of the main three British banks. In its *Final Notice* to Barclays on 27 June 2012 (FSA 2012), imposing a heavy fine, the UK Financial Services Authority (FSA) stated that there was evidence that the bank had been manipulating Libor and Euribor since 2005. It had been during that year that US citizen Bob Diamond had been appointed Barclays chief executive officer (CEO). Although not found personally culpable for the scandal, Diamond resigned soon after the FSA findings, with a compensation package of around £23 million. During the inquiries he claimed that in 2008 the deputy governor of the

Bank of England, Paul Tucker, had actually encouraged the bank to make inaccurate reports to Libor, but Tucker insisted that this had been a misunderstanding. Following Barclays, the Swiss bank UBS and the Royal Bank of Scotland were also found guilty of Libor rigging. Fines awarded against the three in the UK and US combined amounted to £1.6 billion (BBC 2013). Fines of £1.7 billion from UK and US regulators against the German Deutsche Bank followed in 2015 and were particularly high because, according to the UK Financial Conduct Authority, the bank had misled its investigations (Financial Conduct Authority 2015; Treanor 2015).

Considerably larger even than the Libor and Euribor scandal has been the similar exercise of rigging the international currency exchange system, Forex. Transactions in Forex amount to six times the global economy each year. This is another completely unregulated market, where groups of traders working for the world's leading banks have had the power to determine the rates at which national currencies are exchanged. Equipping each other with information about how the current pattern of orders for currencies was developing, they could anticipate how the price would move over the next few minutes, and then decide to buy or sell ahead of the flow. The profit they would make was at the direct expense of the clients for whom they were ostensibly working, and who remained unconscious of what was going on. Although the behaviour involved is very similar to that involved in the Libor and Euribor cases, and although banking leaders had solemnly declared that they had put an end to such conduct after those scandals, the Forex manipulations continued for some years after the earlier exposures and were not acted on by the banks themselves. This scandal involved at least fifteen major banks. In addition to Barclays and UBS again, Citigroup, Deutsche Bank, Goldman Sachs and JPMorgan Chase were among those implicated. None of these can be written off as shadowy marginal figures; they are the heart of the global financial system. In November 2014 courts in Switzerland, the UK and US imposed fines of

£2.6 billion on some of them, albeit after 'negotiation' with the banks themselves, and at the time of writing further cases remain to be resolved (Guthrie 2014). Given that such a high proportion of global banks was involved, it is likely that they will gradually be able to recoup the cost of the fines through higher charges to the customers whom they had cheated. The only alternative is for bank shareholders to take the hit, but unlike customers they do have the chance to go elsewhere with their investments. The scandal is a pure case of knowledge corruption at the expense of customers, who cannot use the market to protect themselves, as it is impossible for them to access the information needed to exercise market choices.

Distortion of information has also been used by banks and other financial firms, particularly in the UK, to persuade individuals to take out payment protection insurance (PPI). This insurance is supposed to ensure that loans and other credit arrangements will continue to be paid after the death of the debtor, though payment is hedged around with many conditions. As PPI is designed to cover repayments on loans and credit cards, most loan and credit card companies sell the policies at the same time as they sell the credit product. By May 2008, 20 million PPI policies existed in the UK, with a further increase of 7 million policies a year being purchased thereafter. About 40 per cent of policyholders claim to be unaware that they had such a policy. The sale of such policies was typically encouraged by large commissions offered by the firms concerned to their staff, as the insurance would commonly make the provider more money than the interest on the original loan. For example, banks were found to have pressed staff into selling PPI by offering very large bonuses for success, but also demotion or pay cuts if they failed to achieve sales targets (Osborne 2012). Companies developed sales scripts, which led their staff to mislead customers as to what they would be getting for PPI. Several offending companies were eventually fined by the FSA (Rankin 2014), and firms subsequently faced compensation claims from victims worth several billion pounds. The sums involved have been so great that it is thought that the compensation paid out to customers who had been cheated played a part in stimulating the UK economy in 2013 (Aldrick 2013).

As with the BP Gulf of Mexico case, these scandals have been very costly for the banks and other firms concerned, and some senior individuals have lost their jobs. However, these people have usually received generous compensation packages; and, perhaps more important, and unlike BP, the main banks involved seem not to have suffered reputational damage. The market has not punished them as in theory it should. They remain at the heart of global banking, and in some cases (such as Goldman Sachs) are heavily involved in working for governments around the world.

We have here concentrated on misconduct that has involved the distortion of knowledge and information, as this is our primary focus. But leading banks have also been engaged in other forms of criminal behaviour. In 2012 HSBC was fined $1.9 billion in US courts for laundering money from Mexican drug smugglers and Iranian terrorists. Another British bank, Standard Chartered, was found guilty in US courts of money laundering for Iran, Sudan, Libya and Burma (Mazur 2013).

Are the risks of fines and transient criticism for dishonesty and illegal behaviour just part of the calculations banks make, like any other business cost? Will they have concluded from this string of exposures and fines that they need to change their behaviour, or that it was still worth while to have suffered the transient costs and criticisms, because they had earned so much during the heyday of the scandals, could usually pass the cost of fines on to customers, and remedy any reputational damage with some advertisements? Alex Brummer, financial correspondent of the right-leaning UK newspaper the *Daily Mail*, argues in his *Bad Banks: Greed, Incompetence and the Next Global Crisis* (2014) that, as the last part of his subtitle implies, sanctions and government responses have not been strong enough, and that both scandalous behaviour and the recklessness that produced the

2007–8 financial crisis will be resumed, leading to further crises.

The archbishop of Canterbury, Justin Welby, himself a former oil industry executive, has argued that 'At the heart of good banks have to be good people' (Cantuar 2013). This raises major issues. It is of course the assumption behind the 'My word is my bond' motto, which in turn supported the totally unregulated Libor based on trust. It is not, however, an assumption that lies at the heart of neoliberal economic and rational choice theories, which consider that individuals should do all they can to maximize their interests, uninhibited by moral concerns that might lead them to deprive shareholders of maximum profits. It is up to the market to punish the corruption and distortion of information and knowledge. If it fails to do so, then there is no market in honesty. In that case, since the market is the only yardstick of value, honesty can have no value, and the rational individual should not have it as part of his or her repertoire of behaviour.

The part of the capitalist economy that is most directly concerned with the integrity of information is the mass media. In many countries there is concern over systematic political biases in mass media that produce distortions in the presentation of news and decisions on priorities. That bias should exist is part of the give and take of liberal democratic politics; but that assumes that a plurality of political positions have a reasonable chance of gaining access to media outlets. If bias becomes systematic – that is, if there are strong factors giving one type of political bias privileged access – then the mass media may become implicated in systematic distortion. This does occur, because very large concentrations of wealth are needed to run major newspapers or radio and television channels, and very wealthy people have distinctive political interests: they do not want public opinion to focus on issues of inequality; nor do they want it to favour taxing the rich. Privately owned mass media are therefore likely to be involved in systematic distortion of politically relevant information. Such media will only avoid a sustained bias towards the interests of the very wealthy if they are owned by trusts that limit owners' interference, or by critical political movements able to pool enough resources to own media outlets, or by wealthy individuals who happen to dissent from a strategy of supporting the interests of individuals like themselves. In European countries these issues are most likely to affect print media, as radio and television are in various kinds of public ownership; some of the issues raised by this will be discussed further in chapter 5. For present purposes we concentrate on private ownership.

Occasionally, issues of distortion in mass media pose particularly acute problems that attract wider notice. A notable case concerned the use of phone hacking and other illegal methods by newspapers based in the UK (Davies 2014). This was not a question of political bias, but of the use of illegally gathered information in order to produce news stories about individuals, often celebrities but sometimes also ordinary people caught up in stressful events. On 9 July 2009 a correspondent of the *Guardian* newspaper, Nick Davies, wrote an article alleging that another newspaper, the *News of the World*, was using illegal phone hacking and that the Metropolitan Police had decided not to pursue the case (Davies 2009). The response of the Press Complaints Council, the newspaper industry's own body set up to regulate its ethical standards, was to condemn the *Guardian*. It did not investigate Davies's own allegations. Two years later, on 5 July 2011, the *Guardian* made a new allegation, that in 2002 journalists at the *News of the World* had hacked the mobile phone of a murdered girl, leading the police and her family to believe that her phone was still being used and that she might still be alive. This unleashed a torrent of public and political anger. In addition to phone hacking, there were now complaints at the publication of distorted and false attacks on individuals, most prominently the parents of a small girl who had disappeared while on holiday in Portugal, and a school teacher falsely accused of having murdered a young woman. Parliament appointed a committee of inquiry led by

Lord Justice Leveson, which reported in November 2012 (House of Commons 2012).

The Leveson Report revealed in parts of the British press a culture of disregard for law in news gathering, and a willingness to attack the reputations of individuals regardless of truth. An example of this was the use of phone hacking of the kind earlier alleged by Nick Davies. This had not been, as the newspapers concerned claimed, the irresponsible action of a few rogue reporters, but systematic practice. Most of the criticism centred on the *News of the World* and the wider media empire of which it was part, News Corp, owned by the former Australian, now US citizen, Rupert Murdoch. But several other corporations were also found to have engaged in these practices. Once again, none of these were fringe organs, but the heart of the British and global newspaper world.

Many issues were raised by these events, but only two are of central interest to us here: the incentives given to newspapers to distort information; and the problems of finding means to ensure high ethical standards that do not themselves risk empowering certain interests to impose their own distortions. We shall take up the second of these in chapter 5. The point relevant to the current discussion is that it is the market that gives newspapers these incentives. Although the British national newspaper industry is a highly concentrated oligopoly, it confronts intense competition, especially from new media. Journalists are therefore under very strong pressure to find stories that will attract wide attention, and to beat their rivals in finding such stories. This places a premium on sensationalism, distortion, and using all available means (including illegal ones) to get information, whether true or false. The process is very similar to that confronting financial services staff under pressure to sell inappropriate PPI.

From the perspective of neoliberal theory, if people want to pay to read sensational stories and are not very troubled if they are distortions, then so be it; if people cared about honesty and moral probity, then the market would punish those newspapers that did not share that concern. As with the PPI, Libor and Forex scandals in the financial markets, there seems to be no market in honesty. Who in that case has the right to impose constraints on people's free choice and require them to possess an honesty that no one has chosen for them in a free market? And if newspapers judge the costs of possible fines and the imprisonment of their staff for illegal phone hacking to be worth while, an operational cost to be set against profits, then again so be it.

Onora O'Neill (2002), writing with extraordinary prescience more than a decade before the *News of the World* case, explained clearly why normal arguments about individual freedom cannot be glibly transferred to powerful organizations:

> Like [John Stuart] Mill we may be passionate about individual freedom of expression, and so about the freedom of the press to represent individuals' opinions and views. But freedom of expression is for individuals, not for institutions. We have good reasons for allowing individuals to express opinions even if they are invented, false, silly, irrelevant or just plain crazy, but hardly for allowing powerful institutions to do so. Yet we are now perilously close to a world in which media conglomerates act as if they too had unrestricted rights of free expression, and therefore a licence to subject positions for which they don't care to caricature and derision, misrepresentation or silence. If they had those unconditional rights they would have rights to undermine individuals' abilities to judge for themselves and to place their trust well, indeed rights to undermine democracy.
>
> ...At the very least we have obligations to communicate in ways that do not destroy or undermine others' prospects of communicating. Yet deceivers do just this. They communicate in ways that others cannot share and follow, test and check, and thereby damage others' communication and action. They undermine the very trust on which communication itself depends: they free ride on others' trust and truthfulness.

This distinction between freedoms appropriate to individuals and those appropriate to large, powerful organizations is an example of that distinction between (neo)liberalism and corporate neoliberalism that appears at several points in the present discussion.

The wider issue of politically motivated distortion of knowledge by mass media is too complex to pursue here in detail, but we can examine what is probably the biggest single example: the attempt by major mass media owners to discredit research into climate change and the impact on global warming of human activities. Again, parts of News Corp have been central. Particularly in the US, major business interests associated with the energy sector, especially those of the Koch brothers, fund think tanks which in turn fund reports by scientists willing to contest the widespread, almost universal, research consensus that there is a link between human activities, especially those related to the oil industry, and climate change (Dunlap and McCright 2012). These reports are then picked up by important parts of the US media, especially the Fox network of television news channels, owned by Murdoch, and presented as findings of superior status to those of virtually all other experts who have studied these issues. This kind of criticism of science can have considerable success among an American public, many of whom are already suspicious of scientific findings that challenge literal interpretations of the Bible (Hmielowski et al. 2014).

Control Over the Generation and Dissemination of Knowledge

The case of climate change brings us to a further form that can be taken by the corruption of knowledge in the interests of corporate profit: control of the sponsorship of research. There were elements of this in the Gulf of Mexico case that we have already discussed. BP donated $500 million for independent research into the consequences of the disaster, but it appears from leaked emails publicized by the

Guardian in April 2011 that it then tried – unsuccessfully – to influence the work that the scientists would do (Goldenberg 2011).

Far more systematic is the role of pharmaceuticals corporations in medical research. A scandal concerning Tamiflu, a medicine designed to combat influenza, brought this issue to light. Tamiflu was developed by the global Swiss pharmaceuticals firm Hoffman La Roche. Trial results published by the firm suggested considerable effectiveness, and the drug was formally recommended to governments around the world by the World Health Organization. The UK government, for example, invested £424 million in a stockpile for the NHS. An international medical research charity, the Cochrane Library, which specializes in systematic reviews of drugs trials, decided to study Tamiflu, and managed to acquire the results of unpublished trials by the firm. The overall result was that the drug seemed to be of little use in limiting the symptoms and in particular the spread of influenza (Chivers 2014; Goldacre 2014). The Cochrane study suggests that Roche had allowed publication of only positive test results.

The *Guardian*'s correspondent and medical practitioner, Ben Goldacre (2012), had been campaigning for some years about the problem of the suppression of research findings by leading pharmaceuticals firms, but it was only the Tamiflu scandal that brought him widespread attention. Other examples had included an anti-depressant drug Seroxat, developed by GlaxoSmithKline, who had not publicized trial evidence that the drug was associated with teenage suicide; and a treatment for rheumatoid arthritis, Vioxx, produced by Merck, who had not reported on the risk of heart attack associated with it. Until Vioxx was withdrawn in 2005 it is estimated to have caused between 90,000 and 140,000 deaths worldwide (Chivers 2014).

More generally, in 2003 the *BMJ* had published a systematic review of the pharmaceutical industry's involvement in research (Lexchin et al. 2003), which reported that companies' own research was less likely to be released for publication in academic journals than that by non-commercial research institutes, and that the research that was published was more likely to present favourable results, though there was no evidence that the research itself was of inferior quality. The article suggested that the issue was important, because the industry was responsible for a growing proportion of research (in the US, for example, it already accounted for more than the country's National Institutes of Health). In 2012 Goldacre published his book, which also pointed to the growing role of companies in sponsoring both product research and doctors' continuing education. Often research reports were 'ghosted' by corporate employees, with academics then being asked to put their own names to them.

A leading role in monitoring pharmaceuticals firms' suppression of research results has been played by Steven Nissen, a leading cardiologist at the Cleveland Clinic in Cleveland, Ohio (Washburn 2007). He was the first to alert the public to the dangers of Vioxx, in 2001. Then, in 2006, he discovered concealed research findings about a Glaxo anti-depressant drug, Paxil, which like Seroxat had been associated with teenage suicide. Settling a lawsuit in relation to this, Glaxo agreed to publish all its other suppressed trial results, including those reporting an association between heart attacks and the anti-diabetes drug Avandia. Soon after Nissen published his results, the US Food and Drug Administration (FDA) reported that it had found similar outcomes and imposed bans on Paxil. At a subsequent Congressional inquiry into why the FDA had not acted before, it emerged that an FDA researcher had reported the findings, but that her managerial superiors had responded by removing her from the project.

What matters most about this issue is the changing balance between corporate and other funding of academic research. In several countries an increasing share of universities' research funding comes from corporations – partly because the enormous growth in research possibilities has outstripped governments' perceptions of what they ought to spend on science, partly because of neoliberals' ideological preference for corporations over governments. The lead has been taken here by US corporations and universities, ever since the Bayh–Dole Act of 1980 enabled universities to own and commercialize government-funded research in partnership with corporations. This has had remarkably positive effects for US global research leadership, but it has also removed earlier inhibitions about the role that profit-maximizing firms might play in influencing research outcomes. It would seem that they largely do this not by interfering in research itself, but by affecting what is published and what suppressed. As a growing proportion of research is funded this way, we should expect a concomitant increase in distortion. One case concerned research at the University of Zurich sponsored by the tobacco firm Philip Morris International. The firm has been campaigning against moves by the Australian and some other governments to require tobacco products to be sold in plain wrappers. The Zurich research suggested that this approach was unsuccessful in reducing smoking. Other scientists and a Swiss anti-smoking campaign organization have claimed to find several defects in the research, which was not peer-reviewed, designed to support Philip Morris's case (Laverty et al. 2014).

Privatization of the Public Good of Knowledge

Often leading on from the issue of corporate influence over the reporting of research, firms may seek to acquire ownership over knowledge. This raises some very difficult issues. In general, knowledge is a public good; its general accessibility is fundamental to its value. For example, the atomic table is a form of classification of chemical elements, built up over decades by large numbers of scientists, the use of which is of fundamental value in chemical research. If a single corporation had ended up owning the atomic table, it would have made colossal monopoly profits, charging every scientist who wanted to use it. Many scientists would not have been able to afford to buy it, and many advances in chemistry would not have taken place. The same is true of the alphabet; it was originally devised by monastic scholars, but is available to all. If it were owned by a corporation, not only would we have to pay a fee every time we wanted to produce a written text, but the corporation concerned would be able to change the alphabet from time to time, requiring printing firms and others to buy whole new sets of characters. This is, however, exactly what does happen with the digitalized forms of the alphabet embedded in computer programs and owned by corporations (mainly one, Microsoft), enabling us to produce symbols on a screen and subsequently on paper by pressing buttons on a keyboard.

Public knowledge goods such as the atomic table, the alphabet and many more like them are problematic for profit-maximizing capitalism. The only way that neoliberal ideologists understand how to protect a public good is to turn it into a private one. This is the solution they offer to the so-called 'tragedy of the commons', the tendency for common property, such as common land, in theory the property of everyone, to become therefore the responsibility of no one. The problem is real enough, as the state of tracts of unowned land, common stairwells in apartment blocks and many other instances reveal. The great historical example that neoliberals cite is the enormous improvements that took place in agriculture in the eighteenth century when landlords were permitted to take into personal ownership and to enclose land that had previously been open commons. Neo-liberals tend to skate over the suffering and brutality that took place as crofters and peasants were expelled from their homes and lost their grazing rights, becoming a poverty-stricken, landless population.

Today's conflicts over similar issues are the ostensibly more decorous and highly technical disputes in law courts over the extent to which corporations should be entitled to claim monopoly rights over discoveries they make. There are serious and difficult issues here. Clearly, individuals and firms that develop a major innovative product following considerable investment need a reward for their efforts, or they would not bother to make the innovations. There is also unfairness if an individual or firm originates a product or an artistic creation but other people can claim credit for and sell the product concerned without making any innovative effort and with no means of redress for the originator. On the other hand, when innovators secure monopoly rights the principles of free-market capitalism are compromised, as that system is supposed to thrive on open competition. These dilemmas, securing a balance between rewarding innovation and limiting monopoly power, are at the heart of law on patents and intellectual copyright and fundamental to the dynamism of a knowledge-based economy. They raise more genuine problems than most of the other issues discussed here. No one can reasonably defend corporations ignoring knowledge that would have saved them from causing a major ecological disaster, lying about the interest rates they have been offering on financial markets, or concealing negative findings from drugs trials. It is far easier to argue the case of a firm that has made a major scientific breakthrough and wishes to protect it from piracy. Even here, however, there are those who would argue the opposite, as the debates over pirating recorded music, films and other forms of entertainment show. If a firm can argue that, say, a particular musical performance would never have existed had it not originated it on the expectation of being able to make a profit from the sale of CDs, one is inclined to support its claim. But if modern technology is making available cheap and effective means whereby there can be mass access to the music through costless computer streaming, is it not an artificial restraint of market forces for the law to support the monopoly power of the corporation concerned? Should they not have to accept that technology has moved on, and that they must find new ways of making musical events profitable? Workers whose skills are made redundant by technological change are expected to re-skill themselves and look for work elsewhere. If they resist change they are dubbed 'Luddites', after the agricultural workers who tried to prevent the introduction of machinery into eighteenth-century English agriculture.

Corporations placed in a similar situation are often rewarded with intellectual property protection.

Similar arguments take place in the pharmaceuticals industry, where there are now well-established, but constantly contested, rules about the number of years that a firm can enjoy a monopoly patent over a medicine it has produced. Clearly balances of this kind can and must be struck. A serious problem arises when corporate power and wealth are used to distort that balance, in lobbying politicians and public officials to make legislation favourable to corporate interests, or in dominating law court decisions through an ability to buy the most effective lawyers. Two examples serve to show the disquieting possibilities that exist.

The first concerns genetically modified organisms (GMO), the controversial chemical processes used to make food plants with exceptional qualities, including resistance to disease. Some of the controversy over GMO concerns unproven anxieties about health risks; more serious are threats to biodiversity presented by crops that are likely to crowd out all rival natural species. But a third issue concerns us here: the monopoly power of a corporation that has developed a GMO product. GMO crops are at the time of writing still banned in the EU, but legally traded in the US and many other parts of the world. Farmers buy GMO seed from a monopoly producer, and then also have to buy from the same firm its patented pesticides and herbicides, which are the only ones capable of protecting the GMO plants. Many farmers, especially but not only in developing countries, have centuries-old prudent traditions of providing next year's seed by reserving some produced by current crops, saving considerable expense. Once they use GMO seed, however, they can no longer do this. Either the genetic modification includes an inability of the plant to produce fertile seed, or the seed is covered by patent; it contravenes the patent to retain seed from a current crop. In either event, farmers are required to purchase new seed each year from the monopoly supplier. The issue is similar in principle to that of entertainment corporations trying to prevent people from streaming music and other programmes despite the technical ability to do so. It is, however, more serious than that, as farmers come to depend on a single corporation for their livelihood.

The main GMO producer, Monsanto Chemicals, asserts its rights, not only against farmers who deliberately make their own seed from last year's Monsanto seed, but also against those who inadvertently acquire Monsanto seed that has been carried by wind or spilled from a neighbouring farm. The US courts have fully supported Monsanto's rights, culminating in a decision by the US Supreme Court in 2013 that Monsanto could sue farmers who inadvertently received Monsanto seed that *they explicitly did not want*. The case had been brought by the Organic Seed Growers and Trade Association, an organization of American farmers opposed to GMO crops and not wanting them on their land. In 2011 the Association sought legal protection for its members in the event that their land came into accidental contact with Monsanto products. They won at local level, but Monsanto then stated that it would not sue farmers whose crops contained only 'traces' (i.e. less than 1 per cent) of its products. On the strength of that undertaking, a federal appeals court accepted the corporation's right to sue farmers receiving, even unwantedly, more than a trace of the firm's seed; and in 2013 the Supreme Court upheld that ruling (US Supreme Court 2013).

The Association was being *faux naïf* in seeking protection for farmers from being sued for accidentally receiving seed that they explicitly did not want, and Monsanto was quick to point out the element of mischief. It is highly unlikely in practice that it would go to court in such a case. However, that only makes it even more remarkable that it should have insisted on its potential right to do so, so concerned is it to preserve all elements of its monopoly position.

The GMO case is not easy to resolve; clearly, Monsanto needs some degree of protection of its invention. It had carried out research and produced a new product that did not already exist in nature; but in some of the issues arising over crop patents, firms are doing something different. They are taking a plant that exists in nature, and claiming a patent over it because they have been the first, not necessarily to carry out a chemical analysis of it, but to file a patent for that analysis. Environmental and anti-monopoly activists call this 'bio-piracy', because they argue that firms are, solely by describing a product found in nature and patenting that description, able to secure monopoly rights over something to which there had previously been open access. Monsanto have also been involved in cases of this kind. For example, the firm was granted an EU patent covering certain virus-resistant traits of melons. The melons originated in India and were registered in international seed banks. All Monsanto had done was to use conventional breeding techniques to transfer the virus-resistant genes to other types of melon. European law prohibits patenting conventional breeding, so the technique itself was not at issue; only the character-istics of the Indian melons. In February 2012 two non-governmental organizations, Navdanya and No Patent on Seeds, together with another agricultural chemicals firm, Bayer CropScience, appealed against the award of the patent. At the time of writing the case is still to be resolved.

The most famous incident of this kind concerned the attempt by a US company, RiceTec, to patent the term 'basmati rice' (Rai 2001). The name basmati rice has been used in India and Pakistan since time immemorial, and was treated as a generic name, so no one in those countries had tried to patent it. However, in 1997 RiceTec applied for a US patent on the grounds that it produced rice using that name by crossing basmati rice with another variety, and wished to protect against use of the name by other firms. A US court awarded the patent, giving RiceTec monopoly use of the name basmati for rice sales throughout the world, except within India and Pakistan. The effect on the export efforts of Indian and Pakistani farmers of this attempt at an abstract form of enclosure movement could well have been similar to the impact on the livelihoods of poor British farmers of the physical enclosure movement of the late eight-eenth century. RiceTec had not invented basmati rice; it was seeking to appropriate the traditional name for its own cross-breed. There was a storm of protest from the Indian government, and the issue was prominent in the angry demonstrations against the nature of the global trading regime that took place at the World Trade Organization in Seattle in 1999. RiceTec eventually withdrew its patent claim for fifteen of the types of grain covered by the original patent, successfully retaining it for three. The three concerned are all Pakistani variants; the Pakistani government had been less involved in protests to the US government than had the Indian.

In this case the attempt to patent naturally occurring crops failed. It is important to note, however, the initial willingness of US patent offices to grant patents of this kind, and the need for major political energy to be expended to prevent firms from succeeding. Neoliberalism is in theory committed to facilitating competition. One might expect a neoliberal global trading regime to err in the opposite direction, to grant inadequate protection to innovators in the interests of competition. In practice the opposite is more likely to occur. It is interesting to compare the willingness of the European Court to insist on opening public services to competition (as for instance in the case of Dutch social housing (Sol and Van der Vos 2013)), and to use competition law to weaken the industrial relations systems of the Nordic countries (Höpner 2008; Deakin and Rogowski 2011) with its acceptance of the claims of large corporations to be protected from competition, even to the extent of allowing corporations to acquire monopoly rights over natural phenomena. It is further evidence that the dominant contemporary ideology is corporate, rather than free-market, neoliberalism; the lobbies loom larger than the ideology.

Conclusions

The discussions in this chapter have merely retold various cases that have come to public prominence. We cannot determine whether these are the total number of incidents, and whether eventually various official and unofficial monitoring services will have resolved them satisfactorily, or whether they are the tips of major, unknown icebergs. In either event it must be accepted that in large numbers of cases the market does its job of requiring firms to make proper use of knowledge. For example, if all oil drilling subordinated safety to short-term profit, there would be many more incidents like the BP Gulf case. Corporate lobbying has been defeated in the case of prominent health warnings on tobacco products (though, as we have seen, as recently as 2014 the Australian government, among others, was still being threatened by Philip Morris, the largest US cigarette manufacturer, over that issue). Several governments and the European Commission are strongly pursuing rights to open internet access to the contents of journals.

Some general themes, however, run across many of the cases discussed here, and give cause for concern. First, all have involved some of the world's largest and most reputable corporations; this is not a tale of sleaze in the economic shadows. Second, in many instances government agencies have been complicit in corporate malpractice, while law courts have been very sympathetic to the cases of corporations seeking monopoly rights. Finally – and this is the main challenge to the Hayekian model of the market as the most reliable provider of knowledge – human agency has been involved at every major point where the misuse of knowledge has been brought to public attention. Whether or not safety is placed above profit in oil drilling depends on the calculations and decisions of managers. Someone in a bank decides whether to lie about an interest rate or not, or to deceive customers about a product or not. Someone in a chemical company decides whether or not to allow the publication of an unflattering trial of its medicines. A judge has to decide how far the law of intellectual copyright should be extended, and how it should be balanced against both the need for competition and the right of the commons to possess some forms of knowledge.

A serious question that emerges from this account is whether, in an economy dominated by politically privileged

giant monopolies, we can continue to accept the amorality
of capitalism. The market is supposed to alleviate us from
relying on each other's morality, as dishonest and other
forms of immoral conduct will in theory be found out
through the competitive process, and the evil-inclined will
be driven out of business. Therefore, as described in chapter
1, it is part of the appeal of free-market doctrine that it
relieves us of the need to trust directly in other market participants' integrity, and of their need to trust in ours. But
what survives of this replacement of human morality by a
system if human decisions remain important at so many
points? What happens if the market provides powerful
incentives that actually favour the dishonest over the honest
or even the morally neutral – as has clearly been the case in
several parts of the financial sector, where such enormous
rewards are to be had? When large corporations dominate
many markets, when an economy is heavily dependent on
knowledge for its functioning, and when the market is so
structured as to give those corporations various incentives
to corrupt or to claim monopoly rights over knowledge, the
situation becomes dangerous. In extensive and important
sectors of the economy, major corporations act with no
moral restraints other than those imposed by law, and even
then they can afford to pay skilful accountants to find ways
round law for them (avoidance rather than evasion, in the
jargon), use their very considerable lobbying powers to have
such laws weakened in the first place, or in the last resort
hard-nose their way through fines and scandals. Although
most major corporations today like to boast of their socially
responsible credentials, their owners and managers do not
seem to behave as though the ethical quality of behaviour
had much real importance for them. Oil companies and
banks found guilty of major offences revealing extensive
corporate dishonesty do not become pariah firms, recoiled
from with horror by other corporations and by government
officials. They continue to function as before, proudly pro-
claiming their brand names and mixing easily in the circles
of the rich and powerful. Few things can better demonstrate

the profound amorality of our politico-economic system than this.

This is by no means the first human epoch where ordinary people have been cheated by the great and powerful; it has been one of the main constants of human society. These issues are important not because of being somehow unprecedented and uniquely large, but because they have particular implications for an age that lays claim to high standards of transparency and accountability. Modern societies possess far more extensive resources of knowledge than their predecessors, we use this knowledge to improve our lives and to achieve very high standards, and we are dependent on that knowledge. But, partly for technical reasons, partly for political reasons stemming from the hegemony of neoliberal ideas and corporate wealth, it is increasingly easy for private interests to privatize ownership and control of knowledge, from actions ranging from its illegal corruption to securing monopoly rights over it, and to persuade public authorities to turn blind eyes to the former and assist the latter. In this way our dependence on knowledge becomes a dependence on these interests, the ethics of whose behaviour are only as good as a highly imperfect market requires them to be.

3

The Corrosion of the Public-Service Ethos

Dep. Com. Rawls: It's a numbers game, and numbers games breed more numbers games...He who owes his good fortune to the numbers abides in them.

The Wire, series 4, episode 8

Det. William 'Bunk' Morland: You turning the world upside down with your bullshit. How are you not in jail?
Det. James 'Jimmy' McNulty: I don't know. The lie's so big, people can live with it, I guess.

The Wire, series 5, episode 10

In the US police series *The Wire* we watch a number of human activities being morally hollowed out by the pursuit of profits and targets. Newspaper journalists distort the facts so that they can impress their bosses with stories that will sell newspapers. The mayor and his team are obsessed with gaming targets for school achievement. And above all the police engage in one ploy after another, including moving murder victims into other units' precincts, to rig statistics and give the appearance that they are achieving their performance targets. The resulting moral degradation of these respectable professions is set alongside the totally amoral, if somewhat more efficient, world of drug dealers, people traffickers and other criminals. Distortion of truth becomes just a routine activity. The previous chapter helps us to explain how this might well happen to newspaper journalists. How has an obsessive pursuit and gaming of targets come to dominate public services such as education and police?

For true neoliberal ideologues the idea of public service is anathema. They might believe in the need for a strong state to guarantee the neoliberal order itself. But that requires only a strong central control point and a system of contract law; it does not imply any public measures in the sense of services provided to citizens by public agencies. Ideally all such services should be transferred to the normal market; failing that, any surviving public services should be provided through means that are as analogous as possible to markets and private ownership. It is in that last respect that neoliberalism becomes implicated in the problems of these services.

The main doctrine that has been used to require public services to behave as though they were in the private sector has been new public management (NPM). One starting point was an article by the British public administration specialist Christopher Hood (1991). Two years later came a book by two American writers, David Osborne and Ted Gaebler (1993): *Reinventing Government: How the Entrepreneurial Spirit is Transforming the Public Sector.* The ideas were later taken up by many governments and particularly prominently by the Organisation for Economic Co-operation and Development (OECD). None of the original authors can in any way be described as enemies of public service. They were concerned that, exempt from the competitive pressure that requires producers in some parts of the private sector to try constantly to make improvements and to be responsive to consumers, public services can become inefficient and remote. The authors sought means by which the public sector could acquire some of the incentives for improvement considered to be typical of the private, in order to save the public sector. As codified by the OECD (2003), the key ingredients were seen as decentralization, management by objectives, contracting out, competition among government units, and an orientation towards consumers.

By no means all of these will be the objects of critical attention here. This is partly because some, such as certain forms of competition among different units in a public service in order to give citizens some choice, or incentives for public employees to keep searching for better and more effective ways of delivering services, should in no way be controversial. No practitioners of an important activity can be left to themselves to perform and receive rewards for their performance without monitoring of various kinds, whether the market, formal regulation or informal, community-level checks. In public services, where markets are usually weak or non-existent and informal monitoring by colleagues can degenerate into cosy cliques, that need is particularly strong. Its absence has in many societies been a cause of inefficiency and poor performance. One of the great contributions of NPM has been to focus attention on this problem and produce solutions in the form of assessments of performance. The following account of some important deficiencies in the methods used should be taken as a rejection not of the whole enterprise, but rather of specific weaknesses of particular techniques, in particular those that have involved the distortion and trivialization of knowledge.

NPM is implicated in this process at a number of points, all of which converge on an attack on the idea of public-service professionalism and its associated ethic. Two particular themes have become problematically dominant within NPM: management by objectives has often been translated as meaning setting quantifiable targets; and the overall idea of becoming more like the private sector has come to mean concentrating all power within a service in the hands of managerial leaders as opposed to professional staff. Other NPM ideas of decentralization and closeness to consumers have often been ignored or found themselves in hopeless conflict with these dominant themes.

If there is a profession that corresponds to the neoliberal ideal, in the sense that it represents what medicine, education, care services, the police and others would be like if NPM reforms were fully implemented, it would be the journalism of the mass media described in the previous chapter – in particular the state of British print media revealed by the scandals surrounding the Murdoch press and other leading UK newspapers. Professional standards were here subordinated to a profit-maximizing management; consumer interests were to be satisfied by publishing stories that maximize short-term readership. There is no refuge in this tough market for practitioners claiming that they work to standards of integrity that represent a value superior to that of making money. Also, if journalists are unable to contest on professional grounds the profit-maximization goal of their senior managers, they become obedient servants. Is this the behavioural model that advocates of NPM wish to see replace the professional ethics of public-service broadcasters, medical practitioners, teachers, university scientists, judges and others?

Without its characteristic commercial pressures, journalism would have the key attributes of a profession. It has a specific body of knowledge that is not easily acquired: a capacity to discover facts and to communicate them and complex ideas concisely in straightforward language. It also has a related and important set of ethics, key to which are a commitment to honesty in the presentation of the facts, and recognition of certain boundaries on the means used to obtain facts. As the Leveson inquiry showed, major parts of the British press have systematically rejected those standards. If the history of British mass-circulation newspapers has anything to teach the public-service professions it is that subjecting a professional activity to market discipline means stripping away ethical inhibitions in the cause of increased profitability. In the wake of the findings of the inquiry and of public reaction to them, the main response of UK newspaper owners has been – successfully – to resist any imposition on them of publicly monitored standards. These same newspapers are among the leaders of campaigns to have tight external regulation imposed on the public-service professions. This stance can be defended by arguing that competition will impose high standards on a commercial press, while nothing protects us from any ethical failings among public professionals providing a monopoly service. However, the effectiveness of competition in relation to commercial media standards was shown in the previous chapter, at least in the British case, to work in exactly the opposite direction: it was competition that led newspapers to take increasingly morally dubious and even illegal measures to obtain stories. The imposition of similar extrinsic goals trumping the maintenance of professional standards must be expected to have similar effects in public services, and advocates of NPM have to work out for themselves whether they accept this as one of the efficiency gains that come from imitating the private sector; or whether they want to draw some red lines around their advocacy of that imitation.

But it might be contested that the imposition of mere analogues of market practices should have no corrupting effect on public-service professions. Surely, since there are no actual shareholders whose desire for profits might distort professional conduct, is it not possible for politicians and civil servants to devise analogues that are entirely in sympathy with a professional ethos? In chapter 1 we briefly explored some reasons why this might not be the case, for example as politicians might for electoral reasons impose goals on a public service that might conflict with a professional assessment of priorities. That in turn raised difficult questions of the relationship between the professions, politicians and democracy that we shall have to confront in the final chapter. Our immediate task is to consider certain more systematic biases in NPM that impose on public-service approaches, derived from the financial sector in particular, that distort and corrupt professional knowledge.

We can identify three forms that this process can take. First is the use of targets to measure public-service performance. Second is the imposition of criteria of success similar to those of the market in services that in part have the responsibility of upholding values that are important but not easily achieved in the market. Third, and rather differently, is the effect on government decision-making and information gathering of the financial sector's privileging of speed.

Targets and the Assessment of Public-Service Performance

The basic flaws of targets and other performance indicators were considered in chapter 1. Their political popularity results from a suspicion, not of knowledge itself, but of its practitioners. As I have discussed elsewhere (Crouch 2011), politicians of many different parties have come to interpret inadequacies in public services as being the fault of the staff working in them, in particular professionals. For neoliberal right-of-centre parties, public employees are suspect as they work without the incentives of the market that should guarantee sensitivity to customers' preferences. Parties of the centre left are more likely to see public employees as their own constituency, but also mistrust relatively well-off professional elites, who are suspected of having contempt for their clients. According to a leading social policy expert who became the British Labour prime minister's health policy advisor, Sir Julian Le Grand (2006), the old model of the professions required the public to believe that all practitioners were 'knights', who could be trusted to work to the best of their abilities because of their professional commitment. But, he argued, few people were thorough-going knights. It was better to err on the side of caution and treat everyone as potential 'knaves', who would behave well only when given a market incentive to do so. Acceptance of this idea necessitated establishing market relationships between providers and their customers wherever possible, replacing reliance on professional ethics. The problem for Le Grand's approach is that it risks throwing out the ethical baby with the hypocritical bathwater, leaving us with professions that have corrupted or discarded their ethical commitment in their pursuit of the market incentives. This brings us back to the idea with which this book started, of paying doctors £55 for every diagnosis of dementia that they make.

Professional ethics are not the same as public-service ethics. Historically the former partly developed in services provided privately, though with a protection from market forces afforded by associational and legal rules that limited competition. There has been continuing debate over whether these limitations protected clients from sharp practices that might be developed by profit-maximizing professionals (e.g. medical practitioners and dentists insisting on unnecessary treatments in order to make money out of a patient), or enabled professionals to charge high fees and treat clients contemptuously. The growth of the welfare state brought several professional services – mainly those in education and health – into the public sector for the mass of the population, joining some that were already in state service: the civil service, the military; in Lutheran countries and in England, the church. There gradually emerged during the second part of the twentieth century the concept of a combined professional public-service ethos. This became seen by many shades of political opinion, but especially the centre left, as a source of motivation that was an alternative, perhaps superior, to the profit maximization of the private sector. This is the assumption that was challenged by Le Grand and other neoliberal policy experts.

Acceptance of the Le Grand doctrine that it was better to suspect people of being knaves rather than trust them to be knights led necessarily to preference for analogues of the price and the profit motive over reliance on any so-called ethical conduct. This was attractive to politicians, not only because it might protect citizens from at best excessively expensive and at worst dishonest professionals hiding behind the veneer of their ethic, but also because of the principal-agent issues it raised. If the principal (in this case government) allows professional staff freedom in how they interpret their tasks, they may pursue an agenda and values of their own that do not correspond to what the principal wants. This can be avoided if, like managers in shareholder-maximizing firms, they are tied to contracts that give them incentives to act only in ways that suit their principal's interests, these latter being embodied in indicators that provide targets for the service's performance. The interests of a service's clients are then served by publication of the target performance of various units (say, schools or hospitals), enabling the clients to choose among units. For this purpose units' performances across a range of targets are usually aggregated to produce league tables.

Despite the strong rhetoric about moving from 'command and control' to customer choice that has accompanied these policies, government here decides the criteria by which customers should be encouraged to make their choices by producing certain selected kinds of information – as indeed do corporate leaders in the private sector. For example, to publish details about children's school performance at very early ages suggests to parents that they should seek schools that push their children early into working for performance targets, imposing a prejudice against educational theories that favour first settling young children into enjoying learning for its own sake. Government thus continues to define what constitutes relevant knowledge, to shape what users 'ought' to regard as important information on which to base choices. The difference between this 'nudging' activity and past practice in deciding patterns of provision is that the selection of many of these indicators is a highly political choice, whereas under former, unreformed systems it was more of an administrative and professional one.

It is not possible to produce indicators that will measure every aspect of a service's performance. When attempts are made to address this problem by expanding the number of indicators, there are complaints that the system has become unmanageable. Such a complaint was made by the Spottiswoode inquiry into English police performance, leading to a simplification of targets (Spottiswoode 2000). But simplification brings its own distortions.

During 2013 it was revealed that extensive sexual abduction of young teenage girls from care homes had been ignored by police in certain northern English cities. A House of Commons select committee had asked the South Yorkshire Police to prioritize this kind of crime, and the leadership of the force had formally done so. However, a year later Her Majesty's Inspectorate of Constabulary (HMIC) (HMIC 2013) found that little had changed on the ground, where police continued to prioritize burglary and vehicle crime. Sexual crimes against children had become a 'priority', but they were not covered by actual performance indicators (HMIC 2013: 15) – which had presumably remained simplified. The report noted that in one of the force's divisions, covering the city of Rotherham, police staffing levels had been reduced. One year later and following further cases, the HMIC found Rotherham police spending considerable time trying to disprove child sex victims' allegations in order to avoid having to report the crimes (Halliday 2014). That last example draws attention to the political motivation of much indicator selection, with governments being interested in only a few 'headline' aspects of performance. Burglary and vehicle crime had been identified as activities that strongly influenced British public perceptions of crime levels in local areas; the sexual abduction of young girls from care homes was not salient – at least not until the South Yorkshire scandals.

Performance indicators are a mix of those things that governments want to measure and those things that can be measured. Some elements of performance are more easily measured than others, and attention then concentrates on the former, a particular problem when trying to measure something as multi-faceted as police work (Collier 2006). Where governments want to measure things that cannot easily be measured, proxy indicators are found for them, or the service is changed so that it does provide indicators. (For example, formal tests might be introduced for schoolchildren at earlier ages than would be educationally desirable in order to measure not their but their teachers' performance. Assessments of academics' research quality privilege the writing of articles over books, partly because Google technology enables assessment of the reception of the former but not the latter.) Achievements that do not provide indicators have to be ignored. Service users are then invited to base their choices on information that has therefore been distorted in various ways.

If we now switch attention to service providers, we can see what happens when they are informed that certain indicators will be used to inform potential customers about their performance. If market incentives are working, three things happen. First, providers try hard to improve their performance so that their unit performs well and they attract more customers; where this occurs, marketization and customer choice have produced an excellent outcome. Second, however, providers start to focus their professional endeavour solely on those elements that are being targeted, as in the South Yorkshire police case. Third and worse still, they begin to 'game' the indicator. This last is the easiest to achieve and brings more immediate results, but it has of course a distorting effect that can be poisonous.

One public-service area highly vulnerable to the first form of abuse, concentration on those elements of performance incorporated into numerical indicators at the expense of others, is education, at both school and university level. Parents are concerned that their children should enter high-quality schools; young people are concerned to choose well-performing universities. Teachers and education managers therefore have a strong incentive to perform well against indicators, if necessary at the expense of activities not included in the indicators. For state schools in England there is additional pressure in that if a school fails to perform well in the league tables it is likely to be offered by government for takeover, usually by a private firm. What schools do is to 'teach to the test', that is, to limit educational effort to preparing pupils to do well in the tests that are used to assess target performance. A British Academy report (Foley and Goldstein 2012) on problems being created by league tables in education and police services cites a particularly strong example that appeared in Texas, where in the early years of this century extraordinary progress was made in pupils' achievements in tests, and in particular a narrowing of ethnic differences. However, when a research team from Rand Corporation came to examine the Texas record, it found that if Texan pupils took other standard US tests, different from those used in Texas itself, their performance was far poorer. Teaching for the Texas tests had left the pupils less able to cope with more general demands made of their knowledge.

Health services are more dangerously affected. In early 2015 there was a reported crisis in the English accident and emergency service. The service had been set a target of treating, admitting to hospital or discharging 95 per cent of patients within four hours, and many local services began failing to meet it. The matter became a major political issue. Local management teams were required to monitor progress repeatedly and to report back to the national centre. Work by the Nuffield Trust, a health service research body, suggested, first, that this time spent reporting was taking time away from the substantive work, and, second, that politicians and senior health service management had put so much stress on the four-hour target that other aspects of emergency care were being neglected (Edwards 2015).

As Onora O'Neill (2002) had remarked several years earlier:

> Much of the mistrust and criticism now directed at professionals and public institutions complains about their diligence in responding to incentives to which they have been required to respond rather than pursuing the intrinsic requirements for being good nurses and teachers, good doctors and police officers, good lecturers and social workers. But what else are they to do under present regimes of accountability?

The gaming of performance indicators

When target scores and league tables are published, or are used by internal managements to reward and punish staff for their performances, further distortion takes place when those involved start to game targets. By gaming one refers to the distortion of conduct, not just by excessive focus on performance indicators at the expense of other aspects of one's work, as in the Texas schools and English police cases, but by the manipulation of data and conduct to give a false appearance that targets are being met. Gaming is far worse than excessive target focus, because it involves direct deceit and dishonesty. For example, if a school places all its educational focus on teaching pupils how to pass examinations rather than on helping them acquire knowledge, one might bemoan a distortion of the purpose of education; but one cannot accuse the school of dishonesty. Very different would be a case where a school pretended that some low-achieving pupils did not exist, thereby depriving them of education, in order to boost its league-table scores for examination success. One way to increase a proportion is to increase the numerator, that is, to increase the number succeeding; but another is to reduce the denominator, that is, to reduce the total number of pupils entered for the examinations, removing those least likely to do well.

This has happened in a number of English schools that have been contracted out to private corporate providers. In 2013 one such school in Oxfordshire, the Spires Academy, boasted of an impressive improvement in its performance in the General Certificate of Secondary Education (GCSE) examinations that pupils take at 16, the first year that the firm concerned, CfBT, had taken over the school. It subsequently emerged that a number of poorly performing children had disappeared from the school's rolls during the year before the examinations. They had been placed in a separate institution, also run by CfBT, which did not enter pupils for the GCSE. The reasons for doing this are not clear, and there is insufficient evidence to demonstrate that the pupils were deliberately removed for the purpose, but it is the case that their disappearance from the denominator benefited the Spires Academy's GCSE success rate. Following the disclosure, CfBT announced that it would cease the practice. Subsequent investigation by Warwick Mansell (2014) of the

Guardian newspaper revealed that 1,730 secondary schools in England together 'lost' 7,500 pupils, while other schools showed a net gain of only 2,000. Some others might have left the country or possibly died, but the large majority of the remaining 5,500 disappeared without trace. Local journalists in Croydon tracked down some particularly strong examples affecting a chain of schools run by the Harris Federation, which is owned by a Conservative member of the House of Lords, Lord Harris. In one case 20 per cent of children 'disappeared' from a school's rolls (Davies 2014).

The opposite approach can also help schools improve their performance: entering successful children for several different examinations in the same subject with different examination boards, or moving children from one exam board's test to another if they seem more likely to do well at the latter. In 2013 the regulatory body for school examinations, Ofqual, estimated that 15 per cent of pupils entered for mathematics examinations had had this experience (Neville 2013).

Another field in which target gaming is having distorting effects on performance is university research. Partly in order to help university managers who understand little of their academic staffs' work to be able to decide whether to promote them, partly (in the UK and some other European countries) to enable national funding bodies to decide which research teams deserve to receive support, systems of measurement of research quality have been developed. These involve devising systems for ranking the quality of academic journals, and then counting the number of articles individuals or departments manage to have published in the highest-ranking ones. As already noted, the approach depends heavily on electronic media for determining journal rankings and counting individuals' scores. Mainly for this reason, book publication is often excluded from assessments, even though in some disciplines the book remains the main medium for reporting research. The importance of publishing in the right journals can have negative effects. Academic cliques sometimes manage to gain control of journals through their

self-recruiting means of appointing editorial boards, enabling them to exclude the work of heterodox researchers,
strengthening the power of orthodoxy and resisting intellectual change. University managers are motivated to allow
departments and sub-departments to grow if their disciplines
have more highly ranked journals associated with them than
some others. Researchers might distort their work to ensure
they can be published in the 'right' journals. When the US
biologist Prof. Randy Schekman was awarded the Nobel
Prize in 2013 he took advantage of the occasion to announce
that he would no longer be writing for the so-called top
journals in his field, because in pursuit of their own profits
they were favouring headline-catching, deliberately provocative contributions and therefore distorting scientists' priorities (Schekman 2013). Interestingly, he compared it to the
bonus culture of the financial sector.

The concentration on quantity of publications in 'leading'
journals is also likely to discourage academic researchers
from taking on challenging tasks. It is usually easier to
develop several articles from routine, unchallenging projects,
and easier to know what is likely to be acceptable to a particular journal, by following closely the pattern of topics and
research methods that it typically publishes. The quality of
journals is usually assessed by measurements of their cita-
tions in other journals. The most-cited journals are usually
those nested firmly within a particular discipline. This dis-
courages researchers from tackling inter-disciplinary projects,
even though these often constitute the margins where the
most original work is done. Those who persist in taking on
such topics may well be warned by university managers that
such behaviour will not help their careers.

A further example of the negative consequences of gaming
and targeting provided by British academic research assessment concerns the vast amount of work that university managements and academics have to do to improve and perfect
their returns to the assessment. Several academics will typically work full-time for several months writing and rewriting
the returns; mock or practice assessments will be staged, to

which professors from other universities will be invited to contribute. All this activity is devoted, not to conducting new research or to improving the substance of research activity, but solely to improving the presentation of that which has already been conducted. The time and other resources devoted to these activities are taken directly from research itself. In this way, research assessment can actually reduce the amount of research conducted.

A far worse example of gaming occurred in a British police force. During 2013, the murder of two children in Southwark, London, led to the discovery that the perpetrator had been the subject of a complaint of rape by a woman in the area some time before; the rape had not been investigated because the woman had eventually agreed that she had 'consented'. Further inquiry by the Independent Police Complaints Commission (IPCC) revealed that the Metropolitan Police's specialized sex crime unit, Sapphire, had a record of pressurizing women to withdraw rape allegations in order to reduce the number of cases reported to them, which would in turn improve its performance scores (IPCC 2013; see also Dodd 2013). The unit had been under severe pressure to meet targets. After September 2009 it was removed from local control, and the practices are considered to have ceased. As with the education cases discussed earlier, one can improve a success rate by reducing the denominator as well as by increasing the numerator.

Media coverage

The British Academy report on league tables referred to earlier (Foley and Goldstein 2012) drew attention to some of the statistical problems involved in constructing performance scores, which make careless use of them highly misleading. For example, school-level education test scores are usually based on small numbers of pupils, meaning that statistics have to be interpreted within wide confidence interval ranges, so wide as to make it difficult to determine whether apparent differences in performance represent real differences at all. The aggregation of scores on a number of different indicators in order to produce an overall single number that can be used to construct a league table is particularly problematic, as arbitrary decisions have to be made about the relative weighting of different indicators.

As Foley and Goldstein acknowledged, these criticisms of league tables in the education field are concerned not so much with the production of data itself as with their use by newspapers. Interpreting this kind of information can be challenging for parents and young people, so a significant industry has developed to assist them with this task. Newspapers examine the performance of institutions according to various criteria, and then rank them, usually according to an aggregation of criteria leading to a simple ranked list, like a sports league table. Newspapers' purpose being to maximize sales and therefore profits, they are more concerned to provide simple ranked lists than leave their readers with decisions among the complex and sometimes contradictory indications that characterize these and most other human activities. Thus newspapers are unlikely to draw attention to statistical inadequacies, and they choose their own systems of aggregation, which means that they often come up with different rankings. In the US, following the introduction after 2001 of compulsory annual tests and publication of test results for all children between 8 and 14 (under the Federal Education Act 2001), newspapers began to publish league tables of individual teachers' results, not just those of schools, paying little attention to the fluctuations that will occur each year in the quality of the pupils a teacher has to teach.

Similar issues affect health services. Following a major scandal at hospitals in Staffordshire in the UK, where far higher numbers of patients had been dying than should have been expected, the government set up a number of inquiries, culminating in one presided over by Prof. Sir Bruce Keogh, to examine fourteen different hospital trusts with high mortality rates. Three days before he was due to report, on 13 July 2013, the *Telegraph* (Donnelly and Sawer 2013) ran a story anticipating the report, under the headline '13,000 died needlessly at 14 worst NHS trusts', indicating that Prof. Keogh would announce such a figure. In fact, his report stated: 'it is clinically meaningless and academically reckless to quantify actual numbers of avoidable deaths' (Keogh 2013: 5). Clinically and academically it may well have had those characteristics, but journalistically it was very good business indeed if it provided a headline of that kind.

The British Academy report on league tables proposed that, given the poor record of newspapers in using perform-ance statistics, there was a case for appointing 'one or more independent (not for profit) institutions' to play a role in monitoring reporting and advising the public when distorted information is being promulgated. One of the report's authors had, with a co-author, several years previously advocated development of a 'code of ethics for performance indicators' (Goldstein and Myers 1996). Nearly two decades later there has been no progress on such a venture. We return again therefore to the theme: neither the market nor the state has found means of excusing us from the search for ethical, trustworthy conduct; and some of their activities may well make that search more necessary. It was suggested earlier that, at least in the UK, print mass media represented the form ideally taken by professionalism under neoliberalism. Much of the valuable work that targets might achieve is being destroyed through their misuse by a profit-oriented journalism. Meanwhile, the professions that had, until the heyday of corporate neoliberalism, tried to keep hold of alternative ethics have been corrupted, partly by the attempt itself to impose the behaviour and ethics of the financial sector on them, partly by their need to come to terms with media distortion. The market-oriented model of public service promulgated by NPM is undermining the NPM system itself – an auto-immune disorder similar to the way in which the dominance of financial knowledge over such issues as safety can produce financial disasters in the com-mercial sector.

The Imposition of Market Values on Public Life

A major problem for neoliberals is the fact that many of the things we value in life are not encompassed by the market, and can either be turned into market commodities only with great difficulty (and often with elaborate state intervention to prevent people from enjoying them free of charge), or can be profitable market goods only for very small elites. The first situation was considered in the previous chapter through the case of copyright and patent law. Here we consider the second, which raises the familiar debate between right and left over inequality. For example, one might point out to a neoliberal that, without state provision of a health service, many medical treatments would simply not be affordable to the majority of citizens. An uncompromising neoliberal will insist that 'not able to afford' means simply 'unwilling to pay'. If someone cares enough about a possible health risk, she should have the foresight to take out medical insurance to provide for the possibility that she might need the relevant treatment and be willing to sacrifice other forms of consumption to pay the premiums. Failure to do that simply means that the person does not really prioritize her health. In such circumstances to tax everyone else in order to ensure that the treatment is available to such a person through a state system is to interfere with the free choices of millions of citizens. The advocate of public health care then contests those arguments by pointing out that capacity to afford varies with income. If we assume a rich and a poor person who both evaluate equally the desirability of insuring against a particular health risk, it will be far easier for the former to pay for that insurance, as he will not have to face giving up other forms of spending for it. If the neoliberal wishes to maintain a moral high ground in continuing the debate, he now has to start defending the actual distribution of income as representing the most efficient of all possible income distributions, because it results from the operation of a free market. In reality it does no such thing, as unless a society had throughout its history been based on perfect markets, or is one in which the inheritance of wealth and social position is impossible, one has to accept that an existing income distribution is the result of a mass of arbitrary chances.

The historical implausibility of the neoliberal defence of the existing distribution is one of the reasons why, despite the general political dominance of neoliberalism, many public services continue to exist, at least in western European societies. The case appears somewhat differently to US eyes where, as Thomas Piketty (2013) has shown, there was historically considerably less inequality of wealth ownership than in Europe. Although that situation has changed out of all recognition in the past four decades, American political sensitivities do not seem yet to have caught up with the country's changed reality as one of the most unequal countries outside the third world. The situation also appears differently in central and eastern Europe, where public services are often seen as a legacy from the state socialist past. But in western Europe major political parties across the spectrum have accepted that the current distribution of income and wealth does not have enough economic or moral legitimacy to justify using it to determine access to certain important services. These should therefore be accessible outside the market and irrespective of ability (or indeed willingness) to afford: mainly health and some other forms of care; certain levels of education and types of culture; some places of beauty and interest, including the general quality of both rural and urban environments; and security from robbery and physical attack. In many of these instances political acceptance of public provision has been based not on the interests of individuals alone, but on perceived collective interests. For example, a whole society is deemed to gain from having an educated population, clean public spaces and a low level of crime. There is always room for debate over how these things should be defined, and over how much of them should be provided. But that there should be such services has not until recently been in dispute.

This is deeply problematic for neoliberals. If the only reliable knowledge is that held in the market (and by illegitimate extension in the leaderships of corporations), it is impossible to develop knowledge of a kind that might inform such a debate without accepting expertise of the kind that Hayekians consider to be dangerous. And yet they have to live in a world where much public provision of this kind exists. How can they assert market values over it? Part of the answer lies in a frontal attack on the knowledge claims of those who assert the importance of, say, public action to combat environmental damage or an education that makes a wide range of cultural experiences available to all children. Both claims, and others like them, can be attacked for imposing a set of prejudices dressed up as knowledge against the freedom of market choice. But this is politically difficult if there has been strong support for the values that the services concerned pursue, and if there seems to be widespread acceptance that these values could not be easily achieved through market processes. The situation is even more difficult if the professions that represent these value systems (such as scientists and teachers) are more highly trusted by the general public than the business spokespersons and politicians who are seeking to undermine them. It is indeed a further difficulty of neoliberals in contemporary western European societies that it is they, the enemies of state intervention, who need to use heavy state action to change accepted sets of priorities in public services.

Neoliberals with political power have responded to these challenges by trying to change the priorities of public services so that they no longer pursue alternative values, but only those that would also result from the market or, more often, the market under corporate control. An important example is provided by the policy of successive UK governments, mentioned in chapter 1, to encourage young people to think about the earnings potential of different university courses, with the intention that this will lead them to pursue subjects believed to lead to high-earning occupations. Interestingly, the key government review that cemented this policy

(UK Government 2010) was chaired by Lord Browne, whom we encountered in the previous chapter as the CEO of BP. His review was produced for a Labour government, but implemented by a Conservative and Liberal coalition, so it represents a broad spectrum of British political opinion; it is also a pure example of practical neoliberalism. Its proposals have been implemented and form the basis of UK higher education policy.

First, the review sought to turn UK higher education into a market-driven system in which customers (i.e. students) are the primary drivers of what and how universities teach, by having student fees, and therefore school leavers' choices, play a major role. In the words of the report: 'more of the investment in higher education will be directed by students' (UK Government 2010: 27). This might seem surprising, in that it places the future structure of what is taught in universities in the hands of people at the point of leaving school and as yet without knowledge of the content of higher education. This was offset by reserving to the central grant system funding for science, technology and health-care courses. There is also a strong element of 'nudge' in the student-driven component, another example of the questionable use of performance indicators. Universities are required to publish certain kinds of data to inform the choice of potential applicants. Some of these are excellent indicators of the quality of education itself, but four are concerned with the only post-experience gains from education on which young people are invited to concentrate: the proportion of a degree course's graduates who, within one year of graduating, are (1) employed full-time in professional or managerial jobs, or (2) in employment; (3) the professional bodies recognizing the course; and (4) average salary of graduates one year after completing the course (UK Government 2010: 30).

This not only strongly encourages young people to look at higher education solely in terms of short-term (after only one year) financial gain; it also gives universities certain incentives when selecting students. A very important issue to remember when considering switching to a market model for public services is that in the market not only do consumers choose suppliers, but suppliers choose customers and are free to treat different kinds of customer differently. Profits are made by targeting some potential customers and ignoring others; that is how firms find their niches in the market. Universities are here being 'nudged', not only to concentrate on courses likely to win quick salary returns for graduates, but to select those students most likely to succeed quickly. In general, quick success in careers comes to young people with well-connected families. The Browne Report placed considerable stress on the need for universities to improve university access for students from disadvantaged backgrounds, while simultaneously giving them this strong incentive to do exactly the opposite. (Similarly, the stress on students achieving success in full-time employment implies a bias against women, should any university wish to game the system to that extent.) Further, to give universities a further incentive to seek a combination of supply and demand that would maximize their financial gains, the report pointed out that universities would be able to charge higher fees if the likely earnings of its graduates were higher: 'Where a key selling point of a course is that it provides improved employability, its charge will become an indicator of its ability to deliver – students will only pay higher charges if there is a proven path to higher earnings' (UK Government 2010: 31). Given that higher charges can also be best afforded by students from families rich enough either to pay their fees without the need for a loan, or to help them repay a loan, universities with high charges will also be likely to attract students from wealthier families – who again will be those most likely quickly to secure high incomes.

This example demonstrates two elements of the neoliberal attack on knowledge. First, the claims of education professionals to know the appropriate content of education better than politicians, corporate leaders and school leavers nudged by the former two groups are undermined. Second, knowledge itself is re-evaluated as that which is of use in the market or to corporations; knowledge, culture and their pursuit have no intrinsic value. Of the two areas safeguarded from the market model – science and technology, and health care – only the latter forms an exception to this; science and technology are protected because of their presumed contributions to economic success.

A major long-term victim of processes such as the UK university funding reform is the claim of public professionals, including professional administrators, to pursue a distinctive ethic associated with their knowledge. As part of NPM, they have been required to learn that the knowledge that they need to do their work is no different from that needed in the corporate sector, and that their distinctive knowledge is distinctive only in the sense of being inferior and less efficient. This doctrine has had a useful by-product for neoliberals. If business expertise is also the best public-service expertise, then the best leaders of public services will be people from private business; and the best places for public servants to acquire the knowledge they need will be on secondments to private firms. Here NPM has enabled corporate neoliberals to dispose of a well-established but increasingly inconvenient liberal-capitalist doctrine: that government officials and private businesspeople need to be kept at some distance from each other, lest their relations become corrupt. If public service will be improved by an increasing blending of the two, as NPM teaches, then that doctrine needs to go out of the window. Acceptance of this change in the interpretation of the relationship between states and capitalist economic institutions is an important indicator of the shift from market to corporate neoliberalism. (For an extended discussion of this theme, see Chang 2007.)

The Priority of Speed

A major advantage of the market over most other complex decision systems is speed. If all relevant knowledge is conveyed in the price, market actors can respond quickly without a need to make inquiries, carry out research and consult opinions. The financial sector in particular prioritizes speed in decision-making, as seconds can make a difference to the terms of a deal. This is the main advantage of the use of computers in finance trading, mentioned in the previous chapter. It was to a large extent the priority placed on speed that led dealers in the run-up to the 2007–8 crisis to fail to discover what was contained in the bundles of assets that they were selling, as every second's delay might make a trader lose out. Refusal to bother to acquire knowledge was thus a cause of the crisis, but that chastening experience has not dislodged the prestige of the financial sector as a model of efficiency that public services should imitate. This dismissal of the importance of considering evidence before making decisions chimes well with Hayek's suspicion of expertise. His main objection to the use of experts in government might have been his fear of a state socialist dictatorship, but its main practical use in neoliberal public-service reform has been in reducing the role of expertise. That may seem strange, given that modern governments seem more surrounded by advisors than ever before. But that is to ignore the very paradoxical change that has taken place in the nature of policy-relevant expertise under neoliberal reforms.

Probably the most important instance of this in recent years has been the rejection of all knowledge apart from the narrowly financial in the EU's treatment of Greece, discussed in the previous chapter. But other instances can also be found, prominently in English education policy. Until the 1980s, changes in the structure of English education (and most other policy areas) were carried out in a manner familiar in many countries: a committee or commission would be appointed with a chair selected for distinction in public or professional life and with no obvious biases, and with members representing a wide range of interests. The committee would commission research, and finally make its recommendations in a lengthy, argued report, which would then be extensively discussed in public. The process would take a number of years. Since the Thatcher government of the 1980s this has changed considerably. Commissions in the education field are rare, and if appointed often comprise one individual, usually with an existing known bias. More often a minister and her advisors announce a policy change in a short document with no prior consultation.

For example, in the early 1960s the Conservative government believed it might be desirable to increase the number of universities. It appointed a commission of thirteen members under the chairmanship of Lionel Robbins, a leading economist who would today be described as a neo-liberal. The commission had a major research programme; during the two years that it sat it generated a major debate in existing universities over the implications of expansion, including of the kinds of resources a new institution would need to be able to compete on more or less equal terms with the existing ancient and nineteenth-century foundations. It finally produced a 335-page report (UK Government 1963). Most of its recommendations were accepted by government, and over the following five or so years a number of new universities were established on the basis of existing technical and other institutions. In 1992 another Conservative government also wanted to expand the number of universities. There was no prior commission, no research or debate. A White Paper was published announcing that all institutions previously known as polytechnics would henceforth be known as universities; no attempt was made to consider whether they would be able to compete with existing institutions.

It is of course possible to argue that this example demonstrates the kind of improvement in efficiency in public policy-making that can be achieved with NPM and private-sector approaches. Instead of a number of people spending time and money on research and detailed discussion, trying to propitiate a wide range of opinion, the country had moved forward to having just one individual announce a major change and get on with implementing it with no time-wasting discussion and compromise. Certainly the new way of doing public business in the UK corresponds closely to the way in which many major corporations operate: a CEO decides, after only as much discussion with subordinates as he chooses. In many corporations this form of dictatorship clearly works, but a number of objections can be raised against its easy transfer to public life. First, corporate leaders do sometimes make mistakes, and at least some of these will result from over-hasty, poorly researched decisions. If they are in a competitive sector the market is supposed to punish them for it through declining market share (though the continuing success of most of the banks that have behaved so badly in recent years leads to some doubt about the effectiveness of this process). There is no analogue of this in the public sphere; general elections do not operate as checks on poor decisions in the same way. The new, rapid-fire policy system practised in the UK does not have a strong record of success. The NHS experienced one major legislative reform to its organizational structure during the 1980s, four during the 1990s, six during the 2000s, and so far one during the 2010s. The English schooling system experienced four legislative reforms to its administration during the 1980s, three during the 1990s, nine during the 2000s, and so far two during the 2010s. This level of legislative activism gives an impression of dynamic government, but the question must be asked why some reorganizations lasted for such a short time. Were they possibly misconceived? Given that reorganization itself is very costly, not least in money terms but also in stress and professional disruption to the staff involved, it must be asked whether more care taken over decisions might not have imposed fewer costs than a pattern of repeated upheaval.

These issues are not British oddities, but stem from fundamental neoliberal NPM principles: that public decision-making should resemble that of corporations as much as possible; that debate and participation by a wide range of interests lead to unbusinesslike compromises. The whole approach is also consistent with the Hayekian principle of rejecting professional expertise as, at best, special pleading by vested interests and, at worst, the first steps on the road to Soviet communism. This alerts us to a paradox that is fundamental to neoliberalism, but which should make Hayekians feel very uneasy. Rejection of expertise and extensive debate leads to a concentration of decision-making in very few hands, mainly the hands of politicians. The role of experts and debate is replaced by increasing reliance on small teams of hand-picked advisors of acceptable ideological principles. These highly political persons monitor the work of professional civil servants, who are mistrusted as being committed to the idea of a public-service ethic. Once again we see how neoliberalism reproduces some of the practices of its ostensible nemesis, state socialism. The system of party appointees monitoring professional state servants was an important component of Soviet government.

Conclusions

Much criticism of the use of targets and other analogues of market mechanisms concentrates on what seems to be an inappropriate transfer of a mechanism from a field where it functions appropriately to one where the analogy with a price mechanism is just too strained. However, the financial crisis of 2007–8 demonstrated that the concentration on single indicators can distort even the heartland of the market economy itself. The problem of finding indicators of things that are hard to assess in themselves applies as much to using share prices to measure the quality of a company as it does to using test scores to measure the performance of a school. But they have the attraction of simplicity. To describe a company's innovation and production or a school's teaching quality directly, substantively and in detail requires both a detailed inquiry and an auditor's or inspector's report. But such reports are long and complex. It is difficult to know how to compare different elements. (So, a school is good at creating a fascination with chemistry among its pupils, but its mathematics results were poor: which of these offsets the other, and to what extent?) In contrast, an indicator such as a league table based on test scores provides some simple numbers. These are all that needs to be perused; any relative weighting among different elements has already been carried out in the construction of the indicators and need not trouble the choosing customer. Comparisons between schools are perfectly, if highly misleadingly, achieved through the league table placings. The system is still expensive, but it can provide evidence on every school every year, and it is not subject to the vagaries of inspectors' biases and skills.

Within a market the indicator (price) entirely replaces the substantive thing that was to be assessed. All trading concerns the indicator, and it acquires a life of its own. From a Hayekian perspective, that is the beauty of the market: one needs no knowledge other than the single numerical indicator of a price. Practitioners not only work with the indicator, ignoring its original link to the thing it was supposed to be measuring, but try to change it without reference to that thing: the process of gaming. Share prices have a life of their own and can, by clever moves in shorting processes, be made to move up and down without any reference to what is going on in the firms whose value they are supposed to measure; children's test scores can be improved by concentrating on the task of taking tests, with only limited relationship to the knowledge that the test questions are supposed to access. In the financial markets this eventually span out of control. The indicators that were supposed to measure the quality of bundles of assets became worth what market players believed other market players would believe other market players would believe they were worth, and so on. What was being traded was not even the indicators, but a whole chain of beliefs about what others might believe about the indicators. It became unnecessary to check what was in the bundles of assets at all, and a very large number of very dodgy unsecured loans were being passed along the chain. One reason why it eventually collapsed was that banks started to realize that none of them were carrying out necessary checks. They ceased to trust each other, and became reluctant to lend to each other – the issue of trust that we considered in the previous chapter.

What bankers had ceased to trust was each other's professional competence. This should have led the banks to ensure, in their own interests, that they had some knowledge of the likely long-term quality of the assets they were holding. But the enormous short-term gains that could be made – both by the individual traders and by the banks for whom they were working – were so vast that it ceased to be rational to have such professional long-term concerns. The market and its associated indicators, we learned from the crisis, depend after all on professional competence to function correctly. But they were sold to the public services as a device for making it unnecessary to rely on this variable human quality. Indicator chasing and professional integrity are difficult bedfellows, and when the former becomes large enough, it pushes the latter out of bed altogether. The rewards achieved by teachers in abandoning a professional concern with inspiring a love of learning in order to boost test scores cannot be compared with those of stock market traders, but the process is the same. The crucial tipping point comes when professionals are persuaded to stop identifying themselves as pursuing a particular skill-related ethic and to devote themselves wholeheartedly to obeying their managers' requirement that they maximize performance on a few indicators that have been chosen for them.

It may be doubted whether anyone outside a small circle of neoliberal policy specialists accepts the full logic of NPM. Another British case illustrates this. During 2012 there was considerable anxiety over stories in two Conservative newspapers, the *Daily Mail* and the *Telegraph*, about a scheme known as the Liverpool Care Pathway (LCP). This was a care plan designed to ease the passage towards death of very seriously ill hospital patients, providing them with more appropriate conditions than a normal hospital bed. Clinical judgements about a patient being close to death can be mistaken, and some patients left the LCP recovered rather than dead. This led to suspicion, particularly among the relatives of some people on LCP, that it was being used to save money on proper medical treatment, and that NHS trusts were being given financial incentives to recommend patients for LCP for this reason. The newspapers took up these anxieties. The *Telegraph* (Bingham 2012) alleged that millions of pounds had been paid out in incentives to use LCP. In response to the outcry the government appointed a committee of inquiry into LCP under Lady Neuberger (2013). She reported some serious cases of abuse of dying patients and the use of a 'tickbox exercise', 'a lack of care and compassion, unavailability of suitably trained staff, no access to proper palliative care advice outside of 9-5, Monday to Friday'. She considered the scheme to be beyond repair, however good its original conception; the government closed it down.

The NHS administration, in its website on 11 November 2012 (NHS England 2012), had rebutted the allegations. It accepted that financial incentives were given to trusts, but insisted that this was done to encourage them to make appropriate use of LCP. It was astonished at the cynicism of the *Telegraph* in suggesting that financial incentives had played this kind of role. Two years later, as reported in chapter 1, the NHS returned to the issue of financial incentives in the treatment of the elderly, offering GPs £55 for every patient they diagnosed as having dementia.

What is really surprising in the LCP story is that the two newspapers concerned, the NHS administration and the government itself were all strong advocates of NPM and of the role of private profit-making firms and private business approaches in the British health service. They should all have welcomed the introduction of incentives potentially to save money in the care of dying patients; instead they displayed a continuing commitment to non-commercial medical ethics. However, none acknowledged the paradox of their situation. This is typical of the way in which these issues are treated. Neoliberal rhetoric and ideology continue to dominate public-policy thinking at the general level; when their implications are inconvenient, ad hoc objections are raised and recourse is suddenly made to the professional and public-service ethics that are in general denigrated and despised as not adequately commercial. What is not taking place is a full reconsideration of how these ethics can be protected and enhanced when the dominant orthodoxy is constantly undermining them.

4

Knowledge for Citizens, Customers or Objects?

The Blob was a 1958 US film about an amoeba that was destroying the world. The blob being invisible, no one heeded those who were warning about its menace. Thirty years later the idea was found useful by Ronald Reagan's secretary for education, William Bennett, who used it to describe what he saw as the vast army of education 'bureaucrats', teachers' unions and academic researchers in education who opposed his plans to reintroduce what is sometimes called 'traditional' education. Twenty years further on some British advocates of similar changes in the UK picked up the phrase. Among these were the secretary of state for education, Michael Gove, who introduced a wave of outsourcing and privatization of English schools. One of his most ardent supporters, Dennis Sewell (2010), wrote:

> The Blob believes that the social purpose of schools is to condition the attitudes of the successor generation so that they provide unquestioning support for equality, diversity and the case for anthropogenic global warming. Mr Gove, however, believes in the value of learning as a good in itself; stresses the emancipatory and empowering effects of education; and he wants schools once again to become engines of social mobility. These divergent visions of what schools are for are utterly inimical.

Gove plans to employ a range of tactics first to shrink and ultimately to destroy the implacable jelly monster. By making schools more independent of both Whitehall and local councils, he hopes to cut off the Blob from much of the funding on which it presently gorges itself. His promised new, free schools on the Swedish model, run by not-for-profit and community groups, and funded by a socially weighted capitation fee, will introduce competitive pressures that will hopefully wean teachers away from pedagogic practices formed in the belly of the Blob and replace them with styles of teaching that enjoy the confidence of the parents of prospective pupils.

Sewell is not an eccentric marginal figure. For many years he was on the political staff of the British Broadcasting Corporation (BBC), and he is now a corresponding editor of the *Spectator*, a major organ of mainstream conservative ideas in the UK. It is important to note that, as in Bennett's original formulation, British Conservative concepts of 'the Blob' include the majority of education researchers. Sewell's inclusion of 'the case for anthropogenic global warming' as among the concerns of 'the Blob' reminds us of a theme mentioned in chapter 2: the opposition of many contemporary conservatives to the broad consensus of scientific opinion on climate change. (It should come as no surprise that Sewell (2009) has also written a book attacking the prominence of Charles Darwin.) After Conservative MP Owen Paterson was dismissed as the UK's secretary of state for the environment (with responsibility for climate change policy), he claimed that the power of 'the Green Blob' had forced the prime minister, David Cameron, to act against him because of his scepticism about climate change (Paterson 2014). This hostility of some right-wing thinkers to the use of research-based and professional knowledge, and even to science in public policy, should not surprise us. In previous chapters we have noted:

- the Hayekian preference for using the market as the repository of the most reliable knowledge, and the

suspicion of attempts to apply knowledge directly in
planning as a kind of dictatorship;
- the hostility of the business lobbies that fund many
neoliberal think tanks to scientists who draw attention
to the role of industry in producing carbon emissions
and other environmental damage;
- the view expressed by some NPM theorists that
professionals who profess an ethical motivation are
to be less trusted than those who follow material
incentives (embodied in Le Grand's (2006) discussion
of 'knights and knaves').

It follows that many neoliberals take a low, suspicious
view of the professional and other staff who work in public
services. Such people are seen as not working for a profit
motive, and therefore not working for the only motive that
neoliberals believe provides a reliable incentive. Public-
service professionals are therefore suspected of being lazy.
Also, because they are – if working at all – guided by their
own sense of how their job needs to be done, they are
difficult to manage and control, and likely to run off
with ideas that neoliberal governments and managers find
inconvenient: 'the Blob'. NPM has enabled neoliberal politicians and managements to resolve some of these problems by making public-service professionals work for
targets rather than their own sense of what needs to be
done; and this further makes it easy for managers who
know nothing of the substance of their work to be able to
control them through measurement of their target performance. But this all remains at second best. The goal of fully
removing the primacy of professional knowledge and professional ethics can only be achieved if their work is transferred to the profit-making sector. Since public opinion
polls regularly report that people in general trust and
respect teachers and medical practitioners more than they
do politicians and business owners, the project has required
the mobilization of considerable public criticism of these
professions.

The cluster of ideas succinctly brought together by Sewell has provided the main themes of the attack on teachers and academic research on education. Medical personnel have proved more difficult to attack as the public has so much respect for the work they do. A real vulnerability, however, has been their tendency to protect each other from criticism and cover up failings. This is why the Staffordshire hospitals case discussed in the previous chapter acquired such importance in British health service debates. It must then be a premise of the neoliberal critique that outsourcing or privatizing professional public services will lead to major improvements in performance, with professionals responding more obediently to competitive and managerial incentives, as the quotation from Sewell (2010) explicitly states. Further, it is claimed that outsourcing will transform public-service users into customers, as seen in the British higher education case discussed in the previous chapter. To consider this further we must posit three possibilities of how public officials or professionals might view members of the public with whom they deal, and of how users are encouraged to perceive themselves: as citizen-users, as customers, or as objects. The citizen-user is a person with entitlements to receive high-quality and appropriate services delivered with respect. The customer is someone to whom things must be sold, if necessary by treating him or her with respect. The object is just a person to whom services must in some formal way be delivered.

There are three strands to this general discussion, which need to be disentwined and subjected to separate analysis, and can be summarized as the implications for:

- the relationship between knowledge and markets in the relatively new economy of outsourced public services;
- professional knowledge when its work is placed within a context of corporate profit making;
- users' knowledge entitlements when they are moved from so-called citizenship to so-called customer status in their relationship to public services.

The New Economy of Outsourcing

Transferring professional public services away from direct management by public bodies to the market is usually presented as bringing advantages of efficiency, stronger control over how professionals do their work, and greater choice for users. This assumes that these professions come under a true market regime of a wide number and diversity of providers. In practice this rarely happens, a fact that affects profoundly how we should evaluate these transfers and their implications for the deployment of professional knowledge.

When an outsourcing exercise is being launched for an area of British social policy, governments usually list 'social enterprises' as the kinds of organization that they would like to see take over parts of a service. Social enterprise is a form of business that very much belongs to the neoliberal mould, as it involves competing non-state providers entering social services delivery and applying some commercial practices to activities previously thought to belong with the state and public-service professionals. However, social enterprises are a kind of capitalism that is not structured for pure profit maximization, and they find it very difficult to compete with standard shareholder businesses. It is therefore notable that Social Enterprise UK, a body representing firms and charities engaged in social enterprise, has produced a highly critical report on the way in which outsourcing is being conducted in one area: the new market in childcare (Social Enterprise UK 2012). It lamented that social enterprises are being completely squeezed out of this field by private equity firms, whose business model enables them to compete so much more successfully for contracts to run children's homes. It also pointed out that three firms dominate this and many other outsourcing markets: G4S, Capita and Serco. Not only does this crowd out social enterprises and other small providers, but three firms are never enough to form a true market. It is impossible to exclude tacit collusion among such a small number, or close interaction between them and government's contract negotiators.

Similarly, the political rhetoric that accompanies the contracting out of schools presents the exercise as providing parents and voluntary groups with opportunities to take education out of the hands of bureaucrats into those of highly motivated enthusiasts. However, in the countries that have gone furthest down this route (Sweden, the UK and the US) many if not most of these groups have eventually been taken over by private equity firms or other owners of chains of schools. In Sweden these have sometimes then dropped a school that has proved unprofitable to run, leaving the old public-service system with the responsibility of taking it back and trying to make it fit for use again. In the UK, the contracts establishing such schools are deals between the secretary of state for education and the company concerned. Provisions in the law governing normal public-sector schools, such as the rights of parents to participate in school governing bodies, can be set aside by these contracts. Curricula are developed by the firms, trademarked and made the intellectual copyright of the company concerned. As a report by the British Trades Union Congress (TUC 2014: 12) commented:

> The appearance of trade marks on the curriculum sections of school websites is anathema to professionals whose work depends on sharing good practice. If there is no bottom-up curriculum innovation teachers become de-skilled and curriculum development falters. The economics of privatisation depends on companies converting into commodities intellectual property (skill and knowledge of professionals), which until now has been held in common, and charging schools for this property.

Again, when large parts of the services of the NHS were offered up for private contracting, government rhetoric stressed the opportunities for local groups of medical practitioners to take local control from central bureaucracy. In the event the great majority of contracts have been awarded to large corporations, many of them with headquarters, and therefore the location of 'local' decision-making, in other European countries or the US. The case has been documented at length by a group of concerned medical practitioners in *NHS for Sale* (Davis et al. 2015). There has also been a similar experience in the UK with hospitals to that with some free schools in Sweden. Hinchingbrooke Hospital in Cambridgeshire, part of the NHS, was taken over by a hedge fund. The takeover was represented by government as an example of how the private sector could remedy weaknesses of public-sector organizations. In early 2015, within three years of the start of the contract, the new owners walked away from it following a critical report of standards by the Care Quality Commission (CQC).

It is very doubtful whether 'market' is the correct term to apply to the form being taken by these outsourcing ventures. The Social Enterprise Report already referred to commented perceptively:

> Some of the largest providers are supplying many government departments and public bodies, with many different kinds of service. They have complex stakes in many markets. It is difficult to imagine them being easily allowed to fail because taxpayers are now dependent on a few companies for a great many services. It is not easy to see who would quickly or easily fill the large gaps they have carved out across public services. For example, Serco operates public transport services such as the Docklands Light Railway and Barclays Cycle Hire Scheme. It manages laboratories including the National Nuclear Laboratory. It runs prisons and young offenders institutions, provides a range of security services to the National Border Agency and other clients, such as accommodation and detention services for asylum seekers; it also supplies electronic tagging systems. It provides maintenance services for missile defence systems and military bases; it provides air traffic control services, facilities and management for hospitals, as well as pathology services. It manages leisure services, administers government websites including Business Link, provides a range of IT services, and operates waste collection services for local

councils. It also manages education authorities on behalf of local governments. Its failure would cause extreme turbulence in public services. (Social Enterprise UK 2012: 10)

Evoking the phrase used about the giant banks that had to be rescued during the financial crisis, Social Enterprise commented that the firms involved in winning contracts to run British public services had become 'too big to fail', so central had they become to providing Britain's public services and infrastructure. Already in 2009 the *Telegraph* had described Serco as 'the company running the country', with £4 billion of public contracts: 'Most of the general public has never come across the name Serco, but the company inspects Britain's schools, trains the armed forces, helps to protect our borders, maintains our nuclear weapons, runs our trains and operates our prisons' (Ruddick 2009).

That firms so successfully develop contracts across fields where they had no prior expertise in the particular bodies of professional knowledge involved or past track record is puzzling. It is true that in normal commerce firms do make occasional extraordinary leaps, the most famous probably being the Finnish firm Nokia's conversion from being a manufacturer of rubber boots to one of mobile phones. But it achieved that change not in a brief period, but after years of research. Such transitions are often difficult and require careful planning, with frequent mistakes, as when supermarkets launch into non-food areas. If we live in a knowledge economy, one might assume that knowledge was necessary to practise in a particular field. The spread of activities of these UK government contractors across areas where they had no prior knowledge is extraordinary. It becomes less puzzling when one realizes that their core business, their core knowledge, is not a particular field of activity, but knowing how to win government contracts: how to bid, how to develop contacts with officials and politicians. On that basis they can undertake contracts across virtually any field where government has decided to outsource.

In outsourced public-service provision we are confronted by a distinctive organizational form. It looks as though it is a form of marketized professionalism, but it is not part of a true market economy, and its core knowledge base is not that of the professions involved.

Often, relatively few people are involved in awarding central government contracts, and in several sectors there is now a small oligopoly of firms successfully involved. Add to this the relaxation of earlier strict rules about the relationships that politicians and officials may develop with firms with which they do business (part of NPM's attempt to enable private business thinking to percolate into government), and one has an interesting insight into how this new economy of outsourced public services operates, its knowledge base and its implications for citizens.

In the UK, and no doubt in other countries that have embarked on this path, a core characteristic of outsourcing is a 'revolving door' between public officials and the key outsourcing companies. For example, G4S (which mainly works in security fields and has some interests in energy metering) has recruited to its board of directors a former UK home secretary (Lord Reid), a former commissioner of the Metropolitan Police (Lord Condon) and a former energy regulator (Claire Spottiswoode). Large numbers of employees of firms in the arms and related industries holding contracts with the Ministry of Defence are seconded to that ministry, while civil servants in the ministry are seconded to the firms (Quinn 2015).

Different firms operate in the increasingly subcontracted world of health, though Serco remains prominent. Ian Dalton was the deputy chief executive of NHS England until he left in 2013 to head the global health division of BT, the telecommunications firm. During the following year BT won £18 million of NHS contracts (Ramesh 2014). Following several years as an NHS administrator, Simon Stevens became a top-level advisor on health policy to the Labour government from 1997 to 2004. He then left to occupy a series of senior posts with a US health-care firm, UnitedHealth, which is eager to win outsourcing contracts in the UK and other European countries. In 2014 he returned to public service as the head of the NHS in England. Mark Britnell had been head of commissioning and systems management in NHS England from 2007 to 2009, when he became the head of health care in Europe and the UK for the accountancy and management consultancy firm KPMG. He now also serves as an advisor to the UK government and the EU on health policy (BBC 2011). His successor as head of NHS England commissioning, Gary Belfield, joined him at KPMG, which was subsequently awarded a £5 billion contract to provide advisory services for general practitioners on how to commission for health contracts – a skill that they need to acquire following legislative changes that have made them responsible for commissioning outsourced contracts (Plimmer 2014). KPMG also recruited Stephen Dorrell MP, former secretary of state for health and former chair of the House of Commons Health Committee, as an advisor as it prepared to bid for a £1 billion contract to run health services (*Telegraph* 2014). Other former UK ministers of health have taken consultancies with private health-care companies after leaving office. When Patricia Hewitt, secretary of state for health in the Labour government from 2005 to 2007, left government office, she became a consultant to two major firms seeking to take over parts of the NHS. Another Labour health secretary (from 1999 to 2003), Alan Milburn, who started the process of outsourcing, heads a board of Pricewaterhouse Coopers, exploring the scope for that management consultancy and accountancy firm to enter the health market. He is also chairman of the European Advisory Panel of Bridgepoint Capital, one of the private equity firms involved in the British care services. One of the firms in which Bridgepoint invests is Care UK, which generates 96 per cent of its £400 million business from the NHS. In 2009 the wife of the principal owner of Care UK donated £21,000 to the maintenance of the private office of Andrew Lansley, the then Conservative secretary of state for health (the department is also responsible for care services) (Watt and Prince 2010).

In March 2013 the *BMJ* (*BMJ* 2013) reported that one third of the board members of the new clinical commissioning groups had financial interests in health-care providing firms. It has been estimated by the trade union Unite that twenty-four of the Conservative members of parliament who voted for the bill to contract out the NHS and care services to private suppliers had links to firms that subsequently won contracts worth £1.5 billion (Taylor 2014).

In October 2014 the UK government appointed John Manzoni to a new post as chief executive of the civil service. While holding this post he continues to work for the brewery firm SABMiller. This fact produced a protest from a group of seventy leading medical practitioners and charities involved in combating alcohol-related health problems, because of SABMiller's prominent role in lobbying against government action to try to reduce alcohol consumption (Mason and Campbell 2014). It was subsequently announced by the Cabinet Office that he would earn no money from his work for the brewery firm while in his civil service post. Manzoni had previously worked for BP, and had been in charge of the Texas City plant in 2005 when the explosion discussed in chapter 2 occurred. He then moved to the Canadian oil fracking firm Talisman, which in 2011 was fined by a US court for repeated breaches of health and safety procedures (Reuters 2012). Fracking is at the time of writing a controversial issue in the UK.

One could continue these lists almost indefinitely, and finding out these connections does not require extensive research. No one is concealing them, because it is part of NPM that such links are to be encouraged, though true market liberals should be shocked to see how their advocacy of markets in the interests of open competition has been interpreted. Whether or not actual corruption is involved in granting contracts within this world of revolving doors, awarding of public contracts to political friends and interpersonal connections is probably beside the point; corruption is unnecessary when interlocking interests of this kind can operate brazenly. The relevant point for our present purposes is to see how a world of contract allocation has become virtually disconnected from the substantive knowledge and expertise required to operate the public services concerned; and even from competent performance of the tasks involved. It is true that some of the individuals concerned are deeply rooted in the knowledge of their sectors; for example, Stevens, Dalton, Britnell and Belfield all had lengthy careers as health service administrators before they entered the overlapping spheres of public policy and private contracting. But, outside their ranks, given that the core business of those involved in these activities has become the fixing and financing of contracts, it is easy to understand why the substantive tasks are often neglected or even subverted – as we shall see in the cases of childcare and schools inspection.

The biggest outsourcing scandal to date in the UK occurred from 1999 to 2013, when G4S and Serco both charged the government several million pounds for prisoner tagging services that they had not in fact provided (Tadeo 2013). Following the firms' refusal to co-operate with government investigations after revelation of the scandal, the police were called in to consider whether criminal charges should be pressed. G4S was eventually allowed to 'settle' the issue out of court by repaying £109 million, Serco by repaying £68.5 million. G4S had meanwhile been involved in another high-profile scandal. It had been awarded a £284 million contract to provide security services for the 2012 London Olympic Games, but two weeks before the event it was found to have made only rudimentary preparations (Booth and Hopkins 2012). The military and police, two public services as yet only marginally outsourced in the UK, had to step in to fill the vacuum. Following the prisoner scandal the firm lost its tagging contracts, which passed to another of the giant corporations active across the public sector, Capita, but G4S has continued to be awarded other public contracts. It has secured £3.5 million of the many NHS contracts that have been outsourced, and in April 2014 it secured a £4 million deal to provide facilities management services for some of Her Majesty's Revenue and Customs (HMRC) sites (Osborne 2014).

In its turn, Serco was found in March 2013 by the National Audit Office to have falsified reports on its conduct of general medical practice services in Cornwall on 252 occasions (Lawrence 2013). Some of the falsifications involved serious lapses of medical care. The firm was required to appear before the House of Commons Public Accounts Committee and publicly criticized (UK Parliament 2013). The firm lost that contract, but has won a further £10 million of NHS business, despite being involved in several cases of poor practice (Davis et al. 2015). Since 2007 another of Serco's contracts has been to run a women's immigration detention centre at Yarl's Wood in Bedfordshire. There were a series of allegations of sexual abuse of inmates by Serco staff, and of pregnant women being held without justification. The women held at Yarl's Wood had not been charged with criminal offences, but were awaiting deportation as illegal immigrants; some had been held for four years. It has not been possible fully to verify the allegations (Townsend 2014). A request by the United Nations to investigate the site was refused by the UK government. In November 2014 Serco was given a new contract, worth £70 million, to continue running the detention centre for another eight years. The Home Office commented that the firm's bid had offered the best value for money (Morris and Pells 2014). Like G4S, Serco lost its prisoner tagging contract to Capita following the original scandal, but has continued to be awarded other public business.

The tag of 'too big to fail' suggested for these firms by Social Enterprise UK seems appropriate. At the height of the scandal over the tagging contracts the director-general of the Confederation of British Industry (CBI), John Cridland, warned Members of Parliament against 'demonizing' the firms by inquiring too closely into their activities, as this could damage the UK (Cridland 2013). Both G4S and Serco have seen their share prices fall heavily since the scandals, but the position in British public life of these and similar firms seems secure; like the banks involved in the 2008 crash, and the PPI, Libor, Euribor and Forex scandals, they have become central to it and cannot be dislodged.

Professional Knowledge in the Outsourced Economy

The rhetoric in favour of outsourcing stresses two priorities: getting professionals to work to higher standards than public service itself requires, because of the gains believed to come from their subordination to management; and getting things done more cheaply, which is believed to follow from the introduction of profit-maximizing firms. That there might be a tension between raising quality of service and reducing its cost is usually overlooked, but it is clearly a risk. A number of cases indicate how that risk might become a reality.

An important example comes from English schools inspection. Since the mid-nineteenth century this work had been performed by an elite corps of Her Majesty's Inspectors of Schools (generally known as HMI). All inspectors had had direct personal experience as teachers. They visited schools, admittedly not very frequently, and afterwards wrote long, nuanced and detailed reports for the benefit of the school's staff and governors, based on their professional knowledge and experience. This model came under considerable strain as school education became increasingly politicized from the late 1970s onwards. Improving the quality of schools became something that every political party had to pledge to do, and politicians also started to have their own ideas about how and what schools should teach, turning these also into election pledges. School performance became central to this process, and from there the idea of targets and league tables as part of a market analogue approach, discussed in the previous chapter, grew. This placed several different strains on the historical HMI model. In 1992 the institution was merged with a new body, originally known as the Office for Standards in Education (Ofsted). Since the start of the present century English educational administration has amalgamated oversight of schools with that of children's services, and Ofsted has similarly acquired additional responsibilities in this field. Its acronym has been retained, but its full title is now the Office for Standards in Education, Children's Services and Skills. ('Skills' reflects the fact that it has also acquired responsibility for standards in adult education.)

The first strain leading to the change was that far more inspections would need to be carried out and far more inspectors recruited if every school were to be inspected often enough to enable up-to-date evaluations to be entered into the competitive process. This would inevitably mean recruiting inspectors with lower levels of competence than the old elite. Second, since these changes were taking place under neoliberal auspices, most inspections would be out-sourced to private firms. Their primary concern with profit maximization would mean prioritization of saving labour costs, as these are by far the main costs of an inspection system. They could do this by having part-time, self-employed inspectors, sometimes school teachers who had taken early retirement. This further implied falling away from the old concept of the high-status HMI. Eventually, as it tried to improve inspector quality, Ofsted accepted the appointment of serving head teachers as part-time inspectors, raising problems of conflicts of interest. Third, since reports would now not only provide help for schools but provide market signals that parents could use when making choices of their children's schools, they would need to take a standardized form, ensuring comparability across schools and providing a small number of clear signals: 'outstanding', 'good', 'satisfactory', 'inadequate'.

These factors combined to produce a radical change in the nature of school inspection reports, which, given both the declining competence of inspectors and the need for strict comparability, had to become primarily a box-ticking exercise against listed criteria, reducing the nuanced advice traditionally associated with HMI reports. Had traditional inspections continued alongside the new form, one could have welcomed the change as the development of an adjunct profession of assistant inspectors, similar to classroom assistants alongside school teachers, nurses with expanded roles alongside medical practitioners, and police community support officers alongside regular police. But instead the old model was just abolished. HMIs, about 250 of whom still visit schools, largely accompany and monitor around 2,000 'additional inspectors', who carry out the actual inspections, reporting back to HMI. The additional inspectors work for (in the case of schools) three private corporations, each of which has a monopoly contract to provide inspectors for a region of the country: CfBT in the north, Serco in the Midlands and Tribal in the south. Strangely, Serco also holds the contract for running schools in two cities in the region where it runs inspections – Stoke and Walsall. Although Ofsted monitors the quality of additional inspectors, it has no control over whom the firms recruit. Some head teachers who had been dismissed from their posts following highly negative Ofsted reports were subsequently employed by the firms as additional inspectors (Exley 2012).

Ofsted also has to cope with the intensely politicized atmosphere surrounding education and childcare services in the UK. This becomes particularly important as successive governments launch new types of semi-private schools that they believe will do better than the traditional state schools. There is therefore considerable interest in how these will measure up during Ofsted inspections, and, rightly or wrongly, there are inevitable suspicions that Ofsted does not want to displease its political masters and report negatively on their favourites. In a critical study of Ofsted, Jacqueline Baxter (2014) has argued that regulation and inspection need boundaries between schools and business interests, and between different layers of accountability. She complains of the lack of these in Ofsted's construction. It is, however, fundamental to the introduction of NPM within a highly politicized context that such barriers will be eroded, partly wilfully (the barrier with private business), partly as an unplanned but likely consequence.

The Ofsted case provides an example of how several elements of the neoliberal approach conspire to undermine professional knowledge: the obsession with target production, seen in this chapter as corrupting the knowledge of inspectors rather than (in the previous one) of the inspected; and the hiving off of activities to firms whose primary motivation is, and is intended to be, profit maximization. But there is no evidence that outsourcing the control of schools to private firms in the UK has undermined the skill base of teachers. A more disturbing example of the distorting effect on a public-service profession's competence comes from the English childcare service, the immediate theme of the Social Enterprise UK report discussed earlier.

Most childcare residential homes in England are today owned by private equity firms, one of whose primary interests in entering such activities is the opportunity it provides for buying and selling residential property. The core business and knowledge bases of financial firms (such as hedge funds and private equity firms) are profit maximization through the financialization of assets, not the substantive business of the activities through which they try to achieve these profits. Under this model, children in care can be moved to homes remote from their areas of origin, in areas where property prices are low. A fundamental professional element of childcare is the knowledge that care workers have of these vulnerable young people, whose parents are either dead, gone away or incapable of looking after them. In principle the English childcare system recognizes this need for professionalism in model fashion. Children in care should have a key worker, and a 'virtual school area lead' who acts *in loco parentis* regarding the child's choice of school, attendance at school and other issues. However, the increasingly dominant private equity model of children's homes provision undermines this. If a child is placed in a home over 100 miles away, as can happen if that is where the firm owning the home finds it most profitable to locate it, it is impossible to maintain continuity in this relationship. Different teachers will now also be responsible for the child, lacking the knowledge of her normal behaviour patterns that is necessary for the well-being of these children. Social Enterprise UK (2012) claimed that this practice of long-distance movement has been partly responsible for the cases of sexual exploitation of young girls in certain northern English cities described in the previous chapter. Its report cited the example of one of the girls involved in the Rochdale abuse case, who had been moved to Rochdale from Essex. She was the only resident in the Rochdale home, but since numbers of different care workers were responsible for her, no one had continuing professional knowledge of her and her habits, and she was loose in a strange town where she knew no one.

The involvement of private equity firms and their motivations in the provision of care in the UK have also been problematic at the other end of the age range. By the early years of the present century a firm called Southern Cross had acquired contracts to run the great majority of British homes for the care of the elderly; the firm was also active in other countries. It was purchased by the US private equity firm Blackstone, who were mainly interested in the value of the properties that Southern Cross owned. It made £640 million by floating Southern Homes on the stock exchange, and then sold the business for £1 billion to the Royal Bank of Scotland (RBS), which in turn sold it to Qatari Investors Group. These successive owners engaged in a sale and leaseback arrangement, whereby Southern Cross sold the homes to the investor, who then leased them back to Southern Cross. In order to make their anticipated profits, the investors kept increasing the rents that needed to be paid on the homes. In June 2011 Southern Cross could no longer cope, and went bankrupt (Neville 2011).

Ostensibly Southern Cross was maintaining the quality of its care throughout these financial crises, since in 2010 the CQC, charged with overseeing standards in care homes, certified that standards at one of its homes, Orchid View, were high. However, within a year it came to light that eleven residents of the home had died in inexplicable circumstances. A serious case review by West Sussex County

Council was sharply critical of professional standards at the home, and of the CQC for not noticing the deficiencies. It called for stricter regulation of care homes (West Sussex Adults Safeguarding Board 2014).

What was the connection between the need for private equity firms to make a profit from their property holdings in children's and old people's homes and the clear lack of high-quality professional care being provided to residents? Scandals have affected some purely public institutions of this kind, so one cannot argue that outsourcing and privatization are the sole causes of such problems. But it is possible to see the mechanisms that might link profit-maximizing ownership of homes, high rents and poor standards of professional care; and it certainly cannot be claimed that outsourcing guarantees high professional standards. On the other hand, problems relating to elderly care in the UK have not been limited to residential homes. Both local councils and firms with outsourcing contracts have been driving down costs by worsening the pay and working conditions of employed carers, which drives down their skill level. Workers providing domiciliary care are normally paid by the minutes that they are scheduled to spend with an individual care recipient. This not only means that they are not paid for the time they spend travelling between clients, but also that they can use no professional judgement in determining whether a care recipient needs more than the scheduled number of minutes on a particular occasion. Their pay has often also been subject to reductions. For example during 2014, Care UK (whom we met earlier as having funded the office of the former responsible cabinet minister) reduced the wages of its care workers by up to 35 per cent, while its chief executive is reported to be paid £800,000 – another instance of the priority of primarily financial expertise over that of the substantive tasks of the service concerned (*Observer* 2014).

It should be noted that until now similar crises have not hit more central education and health services in the UK. This raises interesting questions about the quality of services provided for different kinds of people, which take us to considering the implications of outsourcing for users rather than for the professions involved.

Up- and Down-Market Customers

A fundamental part of the neoliberal and NPM critique of traditional public services is that they treat people as objects, and that promoting them to being customers leads to considerable improvements for them. It is the claim of traditional public-service advocates that it treated them as citizen-users, and that turning them into customers turns them into objects of exploitation. Which view of public service is appropriate will be a matter for the final chapter. For the present we concentrate on the implications of the increasing use of the customer concept in public services, its implications for ideas of citizenship, and how it relates to the thesis that professional services will be better delivered to users if they are transferred to the ownership of private firms.

The public-service user as customer is a matter in which the UK has specialized. For a time British governments experimented with having prisons regard their prisoners as customers. In the official language of British transport services the word 'passenger' has disappeared completely, being replaced by 'customer'. In both examples, the change accompanied the widespread privatization of the services in question. What does it imply if a station announcer is required to say 'Customers for Manchester should change at Birmingham', instead of 'passengers'? Linguistically the change is odd, as it suggests that these customers are intending to buy Manchester rather than just travel to it. Is it meant to encourage railway staff to treat rail users with more respect? That could have been done by training them to see passengers as citizen-users rather than as objects. The only distinctive characteristic of customers among all types of service users is that they are persons to whom things are to be sold. Has the customer concept therefore been responsible for the fact that many British rail stations employ as many people to check that passengers have tickets as to help them acquire tickets? Or that airports everywhere make it easier to go shopping than to sit waiting for a plane or even to find out the gate from which one's plane is leaving?

But these are anecdotes and speculations. For a more systematic account of what happens to users when a public service is trained to exchange its traditional professional knowledge for that of private business, we can take the case of the UK taxation service, HMRC, where implementation of the customer concept has been intensively studied by Penelope Tuck (2013). During the 1990s the service, then known as the Inland Revenue, began, as part of a major NPM initiative, to move to regarding taxpayers as customers. It can be argued that until that time the Revenue saw taxpayers as objects rather than as citizens. Introduction of the customer concept therefore led to increasing consciousness of the taxpayer (or indeed the person entitled to a tax rebate) as a person or organization with needs and characteristics, and the HMRC began to search for ways of extracting tax in ways that suited 'customers'' ways of behaving. In many respects this has been clear gain for both taxpayers themselves and the effectiveness of the Revenue's operations. It has, however, had two questionable consequences. First, an imaginative leap is required if taxpayers are to perceive themselves as 'customers' of the Revenue service, as they are not seeking to buy anything from it. There has therefore had to be some reshaping of perspectives, some application of 'nudge', to encourage them to see things this way. This has had uncertain success. No attempt was made to apply the less incongruous idea of the taxpayer as a citizen with rights and responsibilities; that is a concept without meaning in a neoliberal period. As with the use of fees to turn students into customers, the taxpayer-customer has to be shaped from the top down, not through authorities trying to understand people in their own terms as the rhetoric implies.

Second, more seriously and again with similarities to the student fee case discussed in the previous chapter, the customer concept necessarily implies an inequality, which is inconsistent with the idea of citizenship. In any private business richer customers receive better treatment than poorer ones; there is no private-sector equivalent of a public concept such as 'equality before the law'. Under the impact of the customer reforms the UK Revenue therefore structured taxpayers into a series of groups, ranging from individuals to large corporates. Unsurprisingly the latter are treated differently. As Tuck (2013: 125) comments: 'The corporate customer as a visible customer gains greater prominence within HMRC. With this greater prominence the customer is no longer a passive subject that can be regulated independently of its wishes. It is acknowledged that the customer is an important actant in the regulation process.' This behaviour was explicitly criticized by the House of Commons Public Accounts Committee, which reported in 2011: 'We have serious concerns that large companies are treated more favourably by the Department than other taxpayers. The Department has left itself open to suspicion that its relationships with large companies are too cosy' (UK Parliament 2011: 4). But that is exactly what salespeople are supposed to do to different types of customer.

The most striking example of how HMRC treats corporate and wealthy 'customers' differently from ordinary ones emerged early in 2015, when it was revealed that the authority had since 2010 been aware that the Swiss arm of HSBC, the biggest bank operating in the UK, had helped over 6,000 British residents set up illegal tax-evasion accounts in Switzerland. These were part of an international group of 30,000 such accounts, accounting for £78 billion, details of which were hacked from the computers of the bank by an IT employee, Hervé Falciani, who took the details to France in 2010. The French government took action against French citizens involved, and passed the names of others to the relevant governments. Arrests were made in Greece, Spain, the US, Belgium and Argentina. British names were passed by France to HMRC, but by the end of 2014 only one prosecution had been made; £135 million of unpaid tax was recovered by HMRC through discreet informal deals with those involved. This was at a time when the UK government was running a major campaign to take criminal proceedings against small-scale tax evaders. These facts did not come to light until an international group of investigative journalists published full details in February 2015 (Leigh et al. 2015).

The head of tax at HMRC for much of the time had been David Hartnett, who had earlier been criticized for reaching agreements with Goldman Sachs and with Vodafone that enabled those firms to pay a small quantity of the tax that they had been evading. In 2010 the *Daily Mail* recorded Hartnett telling a conference of accountants and tax officials in India (Parry 2010): 'In my opinion, winning tax disputes at all costs is no way forward in the modern world...We are committed to handling disputes in a non-confrontational way and collaborating with customers wherever possible.' On leaving HMRC in 2012 he became an advisor to HSBC on financial crime governance.

HMRC continues to operate within government, and therefore cannot take us far into the implications of transferring professional public-service work and its knowledge into the private sector. This transfer is usually presented as removing a service from state monopoly into the realm of customer choice. However, outsourcing contracts are awarded by public authorities. These are therefore the customers; the users are simply users, pseudo-customers. The contractors' responsibility is to the public authority, whose interests are not necessarily identical with those of users. In particular, the authorities' main interest is in securing low costs; users' main interest will be in achieving quality of service. These may well conflict, as low cost is not usually associated with high quality.

In August 2009 the council leader of the London Borough of Barnet, Mike Freer, who subsequently became a Conservative Member of Parliament, announced that it would be adopting a 'Ryanair model' for its provision of services (London Borough of Barnet 2009). The reference was to the approach to customer service and pricing of the Irish budget airline, Ryanair. The council would provide very basic services free at the point of use, but for anything above that citizens would have to pay. For example, residents of old people's homes would receive free of charge some basic food, but would have to pay for better. Applicants for planning permission could pay in order to jump queues, as can Ryanair passengers who buy specific seats. Advocates and critics of the approach alike dubbed it easyCouncil, in imitation of the name of another budget airline, easyJet.

Ryanair has achieved extraordinary success by offering what it famously calls a 'no frills' service. Several other so-called low-cost airlines have successfully followed its model, though none quite so thoroughly. Some aspects of the Ryanair philosophy have since been imitated by standard airlines, with the overall result being reduced flight costs for the majority of passengers. The model involves charging a low price for the basic task of getting a flight from A to B (or somewhere near B if access to B itself becomes impossible). Additional services usually associated with air travel might be available, but for extra charges: a designated seat, luggage transported in the hold, on-board food and drink. At one level the Ryanair model represents the market working at its best: if you want in-flight food, you can pay for it, if not, you don't have to; on many standard airlines the cost of food is included in the ticket price whether you want it or not. On the other hand, some other inconveniences that come as part of such a compulsory cost-cutting regime are less likely to be freely chosen: such as restricted legroom, and airports that are often more remote from passengers' likely final destinations than those used by standard airlines.

One person's choice can eventually limit the choices of others. This is most obviously the case with the conflict between out-of-town shopping centres and local shops. It often happens that so many people choose to shop at the former that local shopping centres decline, leaving those (who may well be in large numbers) who prefer local shops without the chance to exercise their choice. Indeed, many people who mainly use out-of-town centres also like occasionally to have local shops for some purposes, but their predominant use of the former may well make that option impossible for them. Low-cost airlines impose some of these restraints on choice. Sometimes, if they dominate a particular route, standard airlines are unlikely to use them too, so it is not possible to exercise the option of travelling there with good legroom.

Ryanair has tested the extremes of its model, sometimes in a tongue-in-cheek way. This has provided a useful real-world experiment in how far one can take the stripped-down approach to service delivery in affluent societies, within which most budget airlines operate, before it meets customer resistance. For example, Ryanair has floated but not proceeded with proposals for having planes where passengers stand for the whole flight, where only one lavatory is provided, or where passengers have to pay to use lavatories. How seriously the airline made these proposals is unclear; possibly they were just attempts to attract publicity. But the interesting point is that they all celebrate an image of down-market service. Most relevant for our present concern with the knowledge base of professions was its proposal that co-pilots were unnecessary on short-haul flights, and that instead cabin stewards could be trained to land aircraft safely in the event of the pilot having collapsed. Regulators were not prepared to accept this idea, and although the airline often responds to regulators' constraints by lamenting that they are standing in the way of its passengers' freedom to choose, it has gone very quiet on this idea (first mooted with great publicity in September 2010). Indeed, when in March 2015 the co-pilot of a Germanwings flight took advantage of the temporary absence of the pilot from the cabin to crash the plane in the French Alps, Ryanair drew public attention to the fact that it always required two persons to be in the cabin. It has to be acknowledged that the firm's cost-cutting does not extend to compromising safety standards, although following some incidents involving three of its planes landing in Valencia, Spain, it was told by international regulators to advise its pilots to carry more fuel reserves.

Ryanair has continued to be a highly popular airline, but it is not appreciated for customer service. It could be said to treat its customers rather as objects. In September 2013 the British consumer organization Which? found in a population survey that Ryanair was rated the worst for customer service out of 100 major brands (Smith 2013).

The story of budget air travel raises some fascinating questions concerning the role of customers that range far beyond the immediate field. How do we deal with all those cases where the exercise of some people's choices excludes those of others? Does it matter if people can pay to jump queues, as occurs when some passengers buy specific seats but others do not? If, in a deregulated market, providers would be willing to compromise customers' physical safety, is that something on which people should expect to make market calculations ('You can save £50 by travelling on this airline, but if the pilot has a heart attack the plane will be landed by a steward')? We are frequently told that one of the hallmarks of high standards in post-industrial economies is the quality of customer service that leading firms have developed. If so, how do we assess the information that one of the most successful companies is rated particularly poorly on that criterion? Does this mean that customer service in mass markets is not really important, and that therefore moves by public services to a private-sector customer model might not bring any advantages to users? This was the issue posed by the Barnet experiment.

Barnet's specific use of the budget airline tag did not prove popular and has rarely been imitated, but the basic philosophy of public services that it embodied has been widely followed, in the UK and elsewhere. Barnet has now outsourced nearly all its services to private firms, the bulk of them going to Capita (Chakrabortty 2014). Citizens contacting the town hall to raise an issue are referred to various different Capita call centres. As a result the council no longer has knowledge bases that it could use to assess the quality of the services it is outsourcing. For example, it employs no lawyers of its own. This goes considerably further along the path to divesting an organization of any substantive knowledge base relevant to customers than a budget airline would ever be likely to consider. This raises a fundamental question: at what point can services that have been seen as citizens' entitlements, where some commercial practices are inappropriate, be changed into tradable market services like any other? This can be crystallized around one example from the Barnet case: the proposal that applicants for planning permission should be permitted to pay to jump the queue would give big development corporations advantages over ordinary citizens seeking to carry out minor works.

Now, in the market economy queue jumping, not just literally but any form of having an opportunity to lay one's hands before others on goods and services in short supply, is entirely routine; if you want quicker, better service, you pay a bit extra. Almost the only reason for using private providers of health care and education is an ability to beat a queue: to get quicker treatment, or to ensure that one's children are taught in small classes. As we have already seen with the case of HMRC, when we enter areas normally seen as those where citizenship is relevant, this becomes more questionable, as citizenship rights assume a basis of equality, embedded in such slogans as 'one person, one vote' and 'all are equal before the law'. These fine ideals are never realized in practice. Votes might be equally distributed, but capacity to lobby governments (which can be far more powerful than a vote) is highly unequally distributed. Legal processes take an egalitarian form, but the richest individuals and corporations can afford the best lawyers, and this must have an outcome in both criminal and civil courts' decisions, otherwise the most expensive lawyers would be priced out of the market. Nevertheless, one would not expect the importation through NPM of private-sector practices into public activities that relate to citizens' rights to offend against the idea of formal equality of treatment.

One might not expect it, but it could happen, as we have seen with the case of HMRC. During 2013 it seemed that the Barnet precedent might be taken further in relation to the English legal system itself. The justice minister, Chris Grayling, announced that he was considering privatizing aspects of court services. Profits could be made partly by charging litigants fees over and above their legal costs for the use of court services. In effect, justice would be bought by customers, not available as a right to citizens. Following considerable protest from judges and others he withdrew the proposal in March 2014 at a symposium convened on the subject by the right-of-centre think tank Policy Exchange (2014), with the provocative title *Privatizing Justice*.

In the US the privatization of justice has gone considerably further than the abortive British attempt. In 2012 the *New York Times* reported on a number of cases in southern states where the pursuit of people who have not paid fines is handed over to private probation companies. The companies have the power to imprison the offenders, and then to charge them a fee for the costs of imprisoning them (Bronner 2012). The paper alleged that the firms and local courts had an incentive to make money by imprisoning people.

Establishing when we should view ourselves as citizens, when just as users without rights as in many of the public outsourcing cases, and when as customers can never be a technical task to be resolved by purely scientific debate. It is ultimately a matter of values, which change slowly over time, and where there is legitimate conflict, disagreement and debate. Until the twentieth century it was taken for granted that medical treatment (such as it was) ought to be bought and sold subject to some charitable provision for the very poor, and in the US that remains the dominant view. That changed in most of Europe during the course of that century, most (though never all) health care becoming viewed as a citizenship right. Today, with the advance of neoliberal thought and with governments under pressure to reduce public spending, powerful attempts are being made to reverse much twentieth-century thinking about citizenship rights, and the border between citizen and customer is being refought. We are being 'nudged' to see ourselves increasingly as customers in a market rather than as citizens of a society;

sometimes the nudge is designed to make us think of ourselves as customers when we are really just users, as when the real customer is a public authority granting an outsourcing contract.

Ryanair have clearly abandoned their plan for replacing co-pilots by stewards capable of landing a plane in a crisis, but it should not be surprising that they thought about it, as reducing costs (increasing profits and possibly reducing prices) in a services industry will primarily take the form of reducing staff costs. And an important means for doing this is to reduce the skill level of the staff employed. As a result there is a decline in the knowledge content of the service that the citizen-customer receives. We can find several examples of how outsourcing in the public services can bring this about, enabling public authorities to use outsourcing and similar devices to reduce the quality of services for citizens to those for down-market customers. However, as already hinted briefly, in making this argument I exclude from criticism such developments as the introduction of teaching assistants alongside teachers, expanding the roles of nurses and pharmacists to relieve stress on medical practitioners, or setting up community support staffs to assist established police forces. Initiatives of this kind free up fully qualified professionals to concentrate on tasks that really need their skill and training, while opening up new forms of professional work to people who would otherwise probably be confined to routine jobs, some of whom might now go on to become fully qualified. These developments have become possible because of the growing educational level of populations. Suspicion about them should focus on cases where they replace rather than assist existing professional grades, and outsourcing provides many such.

That private firms should bring changes to public-service delivery is central to the entire privatization and outsourcing project. That shareholders' profits should be taken from a service where before they had not existed can be justified only if more than enough savings are made through increasing efficiencies solely because of the introduction of the firms. Whether or not they bring improvements or the opposite is itself highly contested, but here we are concerned only with possible implications for the citizenship concept of attempts at realizing efficiencies – or, more easily achieved, simple cost-cutting by reducing the quality of customer service as in the Ryanair case. The rhetorical presentation of privatization to voters always speaks of the gains that should come in customer services if services are provided by competing suppliers, with the role of customer being presented as it exists in very up-market niches. Very little is heard about the possibility that efficiencies will be found by reducing service to pseudo-customers. What made the Barnet venture bold and controversial was that, by invoking the Ryanair model, it was willing to be upfront about this. Less explicit, though clearly behind many of the protests, was the fact that in doing this Barnet Council was discarding the concept of the citizen as the user of public services in favour of that of the down-market customer. This issue is of fundamental importance to public and private life alike.

Conclusions

Nothing in the discussion here challenges the contentions of neoliberals that public-service professionals working with total job security can occasionally be arrogant and treat users of their services as mere objects. We are unable, as are the neoliberal critics, to say what proportion of professionals in various services and countries behave in this way. What we can do, however, is to refute the neoliberal claim that privatizing and outsourcing resolve any such problems. The necessary assumption of these strategies – that they create markets in which professionals are required to be responsive to user/customers – falls on two grounds.

First, outsourcing has often created not markets, but cosy, dubious relations between a small number of firms that bid for contracts and a small number of politicians and public officials involved in awarding them. There are strong grounds for suspecting that many of the firms involved as multi-service providers have now acquired a position of being 'too big to fail' within British public service, which means that they are not really part of a market economy at all. Any arrogance that might have been possessed by professional practitioners has been transferred to the hierarchies of these corporations. Professionals may well have been brought to greater obedience to managements rather than to their professional ethics and knowledge, but not necessarily in the interests of users.

Second, users rarely make a transition to being customers, as government departments become the customer of the services concerned. For these departments, getting a cheaper deal may be more important than securing a high-quality service, which might not correspond to users' interests. Further, when customer status or its analogues is achieved, it does not necessarily bring the implications of high-quality service promised. Up-market and down-market customers always receive very different levels of treatment in the market system.

However, there is no evidence that outsourcing has brought a deterioration in professional standards in major front-line services in the UK. The problems discussed earlier have concerned either less visible parts of services (such as school inspection, rather than teaching), or services the users of which are politically powerless: immigrants being detained before deportation, teenage girls, the very elderly. This suggests a continuing robustness of the concept of democratic social citizenship: services used, and easily perceived, by the great majority of the population are under electoral pressure to perform highly; those provided for unimportant or unpopular groups, or lacking public profile, can be neglected. The pseudo-customer has not seen the citizen off the historical stage; but the latter has restricted scope. This is the oxymoronic conclusion to which we are, on the basis mainly of British experience, led.

5

Citizens, Customers, Politicians, Professionals and Moneymen

As made clear at the end of the previous chapter, I am not claiming that neoliberalism has necessarily brought higher levels of corruption or poorer overall levels of service than other forms of political economy. I also do not claim that majorities of private corporations, target-driven public professionals or outsourced public services behave in the ways described. All I have produced are examples, and examples can never demonstrate typicality. On the other hand, the examples have been related to theoretical arguments as to why we might expect neoliberal approaches to produce such distortions. Whenever instances of bad behaviour are revealed within an organization in any sector it is routine for spokespersons to declare that the perpetrators are unrepresentative minorities. But a vaguely statistical answer of this kind is beside the point. The question to ask is whether the abuse concerned is what one might expect to happen, albeit among a minority of practitioners, given the way an organization is set up, or whether it is completely freakish behaviour by individuals. If, as I believe has been done in the three preceding chapters, the former can be demonstrated to be the case, then a serious situation has been revealed.

That is the charge that I do make: that corporate neoliberalism gives incentives to firms, governments and

professionals in private and public sectors alike that threaten
the integrity of important knowledge. The situation might
be better or worse than in different kinds of society – state
socialism was clearly far worse – but neoliberalism presents
its own characteristic problems of this kind. The charge is
important for two reasons. First, neoliberalism is the regime
under which most of our public life is today conducted, so
its deficiencies are particularly relevant to us. This is especially the case when it prioritizes the kind of knowledge used
in the financial sector over all others, the sector whose very
approach to knowledge and information was at the heart of
the 2007–8 financial crisis. Second, as we saw in the discussion of the contribution of Friedrich von Hayek and others
in chapter 1, it is claimed for neoliberalism that, far from
presenting problems for knowledge, it provides solutions to
them superior to those of public regulation or reliance on
professional ethics. In short, it is claimed by neoliberal theorists that the knowledge necessary for satisfactory choice lies
in the market process itself, not in any human participant,
whether provider, customer or government.

In chapter 1 I proposed five difficulties with this claim:

1 *The attempt to make public services behave as
  though they exist in markets both brings to those
  services an over-simplification of the knowledge
  involved in them and undermines the professions
  that are the carriers of that knowledge.*

We have seen this at work in the dominance of targets as
market analogues for the assessment of performance in
schools, universities, the health service and police forces; it
is the kind of approach that has also wreaked havoc in the
financial sector itself. It is also seen, less dramatically, in the
distortions of adoption of the 'customer' concept where there
are no real customers, only users, or where the idea of customer introduces inequalities of treatment (as in tax collection and the role of courts) or false incentives (as in the US
cases of incentives given to probation companies to imprison).
Also copied from the financial sector is the priority given to

speed of action at the expense of thoroughness – again an approach that has been disastrous in that sector itself. Associated with this is the general denigration of the professions for their working habits, and in a small number of instances (such as child- and elderly care, and English school inspections) the deskilling of some of the occupations involved – with disastrous consequences in such instances as the deaths at Southern Cross elderly homes and the sexual exploitation of girls in some parts of northern England.

2 *Although the market is itself a highly elaborate form of knowledge, heavy reliance on it undermines other forms of knowledge.*

This was seen in the BP Gulf and Texas City disasters and the Fukushima nuclear plant. Relatively rare though such incidents may be, they can be seen as having been produced by the prioritization of financial over other forms of knowledge relevant to business. There are many cases, probably a large majority, where fear of negative market reputation inhibits firms from behaving in this way. But the fact that such incidents can occur shows that the market will not always be enough to offset the negative incentives that the market also gives. Different in operation but belonging to the same class of problems has been the purely financial approach taken to the Euroland debtor countries. We can also consider under this broad heading such incidents as the food industry's campaign against food labelling that consumers find easy to understand, and the distortion of journalism produced by intense competition for readers in profit-maximizing media corporations.

3 *While early theories of the free market saw it as nested among actors who would act with moral integrity, the contemporary form of market theory as rational choice exalts and rewards dishonest behaviour that connives at the corruption of knowledge.*

This was a strong claim. But several of our examples have shown it at work. It has been spectacularly the case in the various scandals and instances of downright criminality in rate-rigging, assisting with tax evasion, and money laundering for drug dealers and terrorists that have rocked leading banks; and in the suppression of the results of unfavourable drugs trials by pharmaceuticals companies. Similarly morally defective have been private equity firms who have taken on the child- and elderly care business in order to enter the property market and with scant regard for the care activities that one might assume were the core business of care. In a smaller way it is also at work in the gaming of targets and other distortions of behaviour among public-service professionals. The worst instances have involved putting poorly performing children into 'shadow' schools, and persuading rape victims to withdraw their allegations. Neoliberals can certainly argue that these cases are evidence for Le Grand's assertion that we do better to treat public-service professionals as knaves rather than as knights, but neoliberals must also accept that one of their proposed remedies – the introduction of market analogues – does not solve problems of professional knavery but only provides new fields for it to exploit. Meanwhile the second neoliberal remedy, privatization or contracting out of services to the private sector, has not only led to dereliction of professional duty as profit maximization has trumped the obligation to provide services of high quality, but has also unleashed a mass of dubious contract activity, where the need for commercial secrecy has cloaked political favours and deals among friends. As with banking, so with corporations active in the new privatized welfare state, being 'too big to fail' also means being too big to be required to maintain ethical standards.

4 *While pure market theory requires an economy with large numbers of producers and consumers, actual existing neoliberalism accepts high levels of concentration of monopoly power. In certain cases this leads to powerful economic elites controlling access to and distorting knowledge to serve their own interests.*

This has been seen, partly in the problems of the ethical standards of the British press, and partly again in the tendencies towards oligopoly and dubious links between corporate representatives and public officials produced by the new economy of outsourcing. Here again the dead hand of 'too big to fail' nullifies many of the gains that the market is expected to bring. This constitutes an inability of the market to operate in ridding itself of poor performers. A different issue within this broad heading concerns the mutually reinforcing relationship between monopoly power and the use of intellectual copyright in such fields as GMO crops and basmati rice.

> 5 To act fully effectively in the market involves being a self-centred, amoral calculating machine. When this is just one among a mass of features of ourselves, this is not problematic. As the market and analogues of it spread into ever further areas of life, however, we have incentives to suppress these other forms of behaviour, and to know ourselves primarily as these machines.

This issue overlaps with the topics considered under (3); when we see ourselves as calculating machines, we are immune to the ethical criteria that might govern our actions. Within (3) we were mainly concerned with behaviour in work roles, while the present topic casts its net wider. It includes, for example, young people persuaded to see their education mainly in terms of the money it might bring; users of services giving up seeing them as aspects of citizenship and acting instead as though they are customers (when they are not even that). Lost with the idea of citizenship are ideas of rights to equality of treatment before the law; instead, there is an acceptance of the trumping of substantive priority by ability to pay.

Citizens, Customers and Objects

It is a central claim of neoliberal ideology that, in contrast with socialist thought, which is concerned with the collective, it is concerned with the individual, and is therefore more human. However, the individual of economic theory is not a 'warm-blooded' human being with the complex and contradictory motives that characterize us all. Economic theory abstracts from this complexity one set of characteristics: our capacity rationally to calculate our interests and to work out how to maximize them. And these interests have to be convertible into money terms, as money constitutes the only measuring rod, both against which all goods and services can be compared, and which provides a strong motivation for human action. For the market to work, all objects of human desire have to be measured against each other, otherwise we cannot make rational decisions about how to maximize. Therefore, anything that cannot be expressed in terms of money, or which would be damaged by being so expressed, has to be discarded. How do I compare the value of buying some new furniture with that of taking a holiday? Easy; they both come with prices, and I just have to compare them, and work out how much satisfaction a unit of each brings me. How do I compare taking a course of study with getting a job? Trickier, as calculating the increase in lifetime earnings a course of study is likely to bring compared with starting work now requires considerable information about future labour markets that is hard to establish. But it is still in theory possible – provided I am prepared to measure the value of study solely in terms that are in principle convertible into money terms. If I start thinking about the intrinsic satisfaction I might gain from possessing the knowledge education brings, then the theory can no longer help me. From a neoliberal perspective, I either have to provide some artificial money measures of my intrinsic satisfaction, or put myself outside the realm of being considered a rational economic individual.

To take another example, how do I compare the value of going to the theatre against that of going to the beach? Provided it is a private beach that charges me for entry there is no problem; just compare the entry prices against the satisfaction I expect to gain from each. If it is a public beach with free access, some economists will be willing to say that I should always choose the beach, as its cost is zero. Stricter ones, however, might argue that, since it lies outside the market economy, its value cannot be calculated; better leave it alone (as it may well be worthless rather than priceless), or wait until it is privatized and the market can provide us with some true prices. And of course, if I start comparing various market opportunities with the pursuit of love and happiness, then economic theory has to give up on me – unless, again, I seek these goals through commercial transactions.

These examples illustrate the main point: that the individuals for whom the market caters are not whole human beings, but abstractions of us. Things go further: the individuals of economics do not even need to be human beings. They can be firms or other organizations; anything capable of making decisions to buy and sell as an undivided unit is an economic individual. In fact, such units better suit the needs of the theory than do warm-blooded human beings, as organizations are more likely to operate in a world of calculable means and ends than are we.

It is indeed very difficult to build theory around whole human persons, as in our wholeness we are too multi-faceted and unpredictable. Some kind of reduction is needed if we are to talk about our needs and wants; it is just an irritating attribute of neoliberals that they make a false claim that their concept of the individual gets close to this wholeness when in fact it is a very one-sided abstraction. To get beyond the limitations of all different approaches to the study of human persons we have to set different conceptions against each other.

In the preceding chapter I have made use of three such conceptions of the person as recipient or purchaser of goods and services: the citizen, the customer and the object. These are of course all limited accounts of us as whole persons. The citizen has civic rights, which enable him or her to participate in discussion and decision-making and therefore not just passively receive services. The customer has the capacity to make choices among goods and services offered in a market. This is a passive right compared with that of the citizen, but it is also easier to exercise. The conflict between these two views of how we relate to society has often been discussed. It is, for example, at the heart of the first two terms in the title of Hirschman's (1970) seminal book *Exit, Voice and Loyalty.* Customers can 'exit', by not choosing something they dislike. Citizens are more likely to use 'voice', that is, to participate in collective discussions about how to achieve what they want. Hirschman's third term, 'loyalty', has been less often used. It refers to the ways in which the firms, authorities and other organizations involved in customer and citizen relations persuade people not to use the powers that these identities give them. Loyal customers do not market-test their choices of a favourite brand; loyal citizens do not protest or make demands.

None of these concepts helps us with the idea of 'objects' that I have used here, though it helps the leaders of institutions treat people as objects if the latter exercise unquestioning loyalty, since I have used 'object' to describe the ways in which the recipients of services can be treated as passive and unable to respond. Neoliberal critics argue that, where people have no choice, as in some (but by no means all) public services, providers have little incentive to bother to treat them well. They therefore become mere objects. The usual response of defenders of public services is to argue that, at least in democracies, people can easily complain about poor service, and if necessary organize politically to seek improvements. In other words, citizens can use voice. Neoliberals will respond that in practice this is hard to do, especially for less well educated or particularly hard-working people, who lack the capacity or time to take action of that kind. Neoliberals point instead to the ease with which a market allows customers to make choices without needing to articulate or organize. Critics of the market point out in return that choices are often very limited, with customers being offered goods and services from different suppliers, but all very much the same.

Unfortunately both sets of criticism are frequently valid, and both customers and citizens often end up being treated as objects. It is likely that the users of outsourced public services discussed in the previous chapter get the worst of both worlds: they are neither citizens nor customers, and the more or less monopoly suppliers of their services enjoy privileged relations with public authorities and may well have reached the position of being 'too big to fail'. Neither citizen protest nor customer choice can make much headway in such circumstances.

For Hirschman there was an interesting tension between exit and choice. On the one hand, if a wealthy elite is able to buy in the private market education, health, security and other services that the mass of citizens receive from the state, the most articulate and powerful contributors to voice do not need to participate in citizenship activities. This leads some critics to oppose all choice in public services, on the grounds that lack of choice will force the articulate and powerful to reinforce the voice of citizenship. But this is not an accurate reading of Hirschman, who argued that where there is no possibility of exit, authorities have little need to listen to voice, as everyone is trapped. On the other hand, where there is no voice (as in the pure market), people have no means to articulate their criticisms of existing patterns of provision, or to explain to providers the kinds of service they would like. In market theory purchasers are passive: providers put things on the market, and purchasers choose from what is available. A diversity of wants is met by there being a sufficiently large number of producers, all seeking different market niches and thereby eventually responding to a variety of different wants. None of this applies to the users of public services that have been outsourced by the government customer to a monopoly supplier.

Ordinary persons stand their best chance of avoiding object status if they can combine the roles of citizen and customer, possessing rights and a capacity to complain and to mobilize with some chance of being taken seriously, but also some ability to make choices. Both these roles require knowledge if they are to be exercised effectively: citizens can be mobilized only on the basis of knowledge that informs them of the causes of their dissatisfactions, the potential availability of alternatives, and the actions that might bring them success. Customers can make intelligent choices only with information. The knowledge needs of the citizen are greater, as more than just a passive selection from offered alternatives is required. This is why a supply of accurate and full knowledge is so important to democracy, and why corruptions of knowledge of the kind we have been discussing constitute a threat to its integrity.

Politicians, Professionals and Moneymen

We next need to identify, not so much the antagonists, as the conflictual partners of these citizen customers. Once again we must remember that we are here concerned not with the whole gamut of relationships, but only with those that are relevant to solving the problem of inadequate, inappropriate or misleading knowledge. Relevant candidates for discussion here are firms (particularly financially driven ones), political decision-makers, and professionals.

Firms active in the private sector have certain incentives to satisfy customers; very few to respond to citizens. But they also have incentives to deceive customers about their products, as in the case of inadequate food labelling, inadequately tested medicines, and financial products such as PPI. Market forces can provide some protection to customers, as firms can be expected to seek competitive advantage over each other by offering customers accurate information. However, this assumes that customers know that there is some relevant information that they ought to have, among the bewildering details of boastful and often unfounded claims made for products by advertisers. The market is unlikely to press firms to provide knowledge critical of products unless the risks concerned are well known. That knowledge will almost certainly have to be generated outside the market, usually in universities and similar research centres. But the knowledge that emerges from research findings is not easily accessed by ordinary customers, and is often difficult to interpret if not actually contradictory. Not surprisingly, even the most neoliberal governments often find themselves regulating products with questionable characteristics. The threat of regulation sometimes leads firms in the sector concerned to offer voluntary information-providing codes. However, these moves usually occur only after knowledge and pressure coming from government and other non-commercial institutions, and often offer a low level of information.

As the goods and services we consume come to contain increasingly sophisticated ingredients that the non-expert citizen cannot be expected to grasp, these needs for regulation intensify, to the discontent of neoliberal thinkers and business lobbies. Further, regulation in the neoliberal sense of applying mathematical tests to ensure that monopolies and oligopolies price their goods as though they were in fully competitive markets is inadequate. It does not deal, not just with information asymmetries, but with the corruptions of knowledge of which firms in markets with limited competition are capable. If customers are to be treated also as citizens, they must have maximum information available to them and maximum protection from exploitation through distortions of information. Powerful forces act against citizens' interests in having more knowledge. Governments, increasingly vulnerable to lobbying and eager not to upset corporations that might locate their activities elsewhere, can be reluctant to act. More disturbing, the increased dependence of university research on funding by firms seeking to develop products is threatening to silence the main source of relevant advanced, critical knowledge.

Meanwhile, it is citizens who represent the impact of externalities from firms' actions. There are cases where people are both citizens and customers, and they may decide that they will put up with the damage done to their shared collective resources in order to have access to the firm's products; but more usually in the modern economy a large firm's customers are distributed widely around a region or even the world. Residents of areas bordering the Gulf of Mexico had little specific interest as customers of BP, though residents of a large part of Japan were customers of the Fukushima plant. It is more likely to be employees than customers who put up with a plant's externalities in order to keep jobs. Neoliberal theory has nothing to say about employees' rights, other than that if they do not like aspects of their job, they should move away and find a different one. In general, however, the role of customer is far weaker than that of citizen in coping with externalities. There are further problems when citizens face conflicts with each other, as when plans are made for some major infrastructure, such as a high-speed rail network or motorway. This may be beneficial in some rather general way to a wide community, but very damaging in a highly specific way to the environment of a relatively small number. All these disputes depend on knowledge for their effective resolution: knowledge about the nature and extent of the threat posed by the externality, or indeed by the intrinsic properties.

As with issues restricted to customers and without wider ramifications, these problems are widely recognized through the whole apparatus of regulation to control externalities, regulations that many neoliberals would like to reduce. But again as with pure customer issues, friendly relations between regulators or politicians and firms, encouraged by NPM, can easily reduce the extent to which citizens are protected by regulation, while universities' growing dependence on corporate research sponsorship threatens the autonomy of the knowledge they produce in commercially sensitive fields. Further, firms' own concern for reputation as 'good corporate citizens' can be undermined by the growing dominance of financial capital and its associated knowledge. In principle the search for profit maximization should lead firms to seek a good reputation, and no doubt there are many instances where this occurs. But where the degree of competition in a sector is weak, where risks of untoward occurrences are rated low, where there is a good chance that knowledge of what has been going on can be concealed, or where it is calculated that a few weeks' skilful advertising can dispose of reputation difficulties, the market will not be enough to help citizens in their avoidance of negative consequences of economic activity.

If customers' main relationship is with the firms whose goods and services they buy, citizens' equivalent is the democratic state. They look to the state to regulate problems of the kind we have been discussing, on the basis of knowledge to which it has access. But citizens also rely strongly on the state to safeguard the quality and integrity of sources of knowledge, knowledge of that kind being an externality for the market. This second question raises problems. In a naive view of democratic citizenship, governments respond to citizens' demands expressed through the ballot box. Citizens, it can be argued, have an incontestable interest in having knowledge of issues important to their lives that is of high quality and integrity – they can certainly not have the opposite interest. Therefore in democratic societies governments will ensure that knowledge of that kind is produced and safeguarded. Naivety is rarely entirely false, and there are very many instances where government behaves in precisely that way. At least since Wilhelm von Humboldt persuaded the Kaiser that science could not thrive unless professors enjoyed full academic freedom, governments have respected and protected the autonomy of state universities. Many governments also maintain statistical offices and broadcasting services that they place beyond their own political reach, often to their discomfort. It is probably the most reliable indication that a democracy has achieved a sophisticated maturity when the state protects knowledge-producing institutions from itself, even when they are in principle dependent on it.

It would, however, be simple-minded not to recognize the delicacy of the balance between governments' need to be seen to protect their citizens' interests in high-quality information and their interest in using information as a political weapon. Public broadcasting media, or publicly regulated private broadcasters, public statistical and economic forecasting services are under continual pressure to please political masters. In advanced democracies this pressure is rarely exercised directly, but will come through such mechanisms as reminders to senior figures in these services that, when the time comes for them to move on to another post, governments have many honours, offices of profit and other glittering prizes to offer to those who have pleased them; and to withhold from those who have been a nuisance.

The situation varies across countries, but it is a remarkable testament to the strength of knowledge in democracy that this neutrality survives and often thrives. Certainly, in many countries state-regulated broadcasting media safeguard the integrity of information far better than do usually unregulated print media, and countries where broadcasting regulation insists on political balance generally have superior broadcasting media in this regard than those where regulation is more relaxed, more neoliberal. Jean Seaton (2008) has identified a very good example in the different political content of Fox News in the US and Sky News in the UK. News Corp, the global media concern owned by Rupert Murdoch (whom we met in chapter 2 in connection with scandals attached to the British newspaper the *News of the World*), is the dominant owner of both. There is some difference, in that in the UK News Corp has been prevented from having complete ownership of the satellite broadcaster BSkyB that features Sky News, but that difference is itself a reflection of the tougher regulatory environment in the UK. Fox is known as giving precedence to far-right political views, especially on such issues as climate change. (It does, though, have to be conceded that it also features the left-leaning cartoon *The Simpsons*.) There are, however, rarely complaints about the political balance of BSkyB, which abides by British regulatory standards of balance in broadcast news media.

These and similar facts should make uncomfortable reading for neoliberals. Their favourite device for guaranteeing the free flow of information, the free market, has, in mature democracies, a record far inferior to both public and other primarily non-market institutions such as universities. However, when I here say 'public' I am mainly referring to institutions of a rather particular kind: those established by the state but protected by charters from political interference; and regulations that are created by elected governments, but which depend for their practical operation on professional staffs, ultimately enforced by law courts. These are public institutions established by state decree but enjoying both de facto and de jure autonomy from political intervention. They are placed at least at one remove from the reach of politicians – and therefore, it can be argued, from democracy. I may seem here to be approaching the same suspicion of democracy expressed by Hayek and criticized in chapter 1, with the exception that he placed his faith in the market, while I seem to be placing it in the hands of a kind of Platonic elite of professionals and experts, the kind of technocracy that Hayek associated with dictatorship.

To gain a proper perspective on this question, we must first note that the actions of elected politicians are not the equivalent of the voice of democracy, even though politicians routinely insist that this is the case. I am here referring immediately not to the fact – important, but a problem very difficult to resolve – that politicians in parliamentary democracies have to respond to many issues where it is impossible for them to establish the will of the people, but to the problem of the misuse of trust by politicians in relation to citizens. From this arises a second and more difficult issue of the relationship between expertise and democracy or, to continue the personalization, that between professionals and citizens.

Democracy and politicians in their place

Whenever a government interferes with the presentation of reality in order to further its electoral chances or general popularity, politicians lose their right to claim to represent the popular will, because they are using their power to influence that will through distortion, which cannot be the same

as representing it. In such cases, democracy has to be protected from politics. I do not mean that politicians should
not be able to present persuasive, rhetorical views of reality
in order to convince voters of their case; that is the essence
of democratic debate if it is not to be reduced to a technical
exercise. Politics has to be about making value choices, and
debates about these are necessarily rhetorical and emotional.
There is a major difference between that debate and such
things as: the distortion of economic statistics to make performance look better than it really was; putting pressure on
national broadcasting agencies to present facts favourable to
the government of the day or to conceal those that it finds
inconvenient; persuading inspectorates to provide reports
favourable to ministers' political friends. To go further, it is
also a distortion of democracy to massage economic performance so that in a pre-election period things are booming,
only to be paid for with a collapse after the election. Institutions that remove decision-making over factors of this kind
from the hands of politicians and those within their patron-
age protect citizens from the abuse of the knowledge available to them and therefore strengthen democracy rather than
weaken it.

As far as possible, therefore, we should place such institutions in the hands of professionals, with balances among the
political biases of those employed if such biases are relevant.
The institutions themselves need to be established by statute
and their professional staff must ultimately be appointed by
persons who have themselves emerged from a political
process. However, the institutions should as far as possible
be established, and their key staff appointed, on a multi-
party basis, not by the government of the day. This goes for
state statistical and information services, state broadcasting
media, regulatory agencies covering parts of the private
sector where knowledge is politically sensitive (such as mass
print media), central banks and of course law courts.

Second, and more difficult to determine, are those issues
where it is rational for citizens to say: 'We have some basic
preferences on this matter, but we are aware that to go

beyond that requires expertise that we do not have; in that case we just need guarantees that the professionals charged with implementing the broad framework that we establish are acting with competence and integrity.' Of course, citizens will probably be speaking with divided voices on these basic preferences; this is where serious democratic debate takes place. Even then, however, democracy probably expresses itself most fully where major decisions reflect overall balances of strongly held views and not just 'winner takes all' majorities. In practice, as with my first set of arguments, it will not usually be citizens as such who either forswear or use their power to go beyond the expression of basic preferences, but politicians.

Some examples will illustrate the ostensibly fine line I am trying to draw. It was democratically relevant and appropriate when conservative politicians and educationists in the UK and US in the 1970s, and in Sweden in the 2000s, raised criticisms of what was called 'progressive' education. This was a debate over the basic values that people wanted to see embodied in children's schooling. For conservatives it is important that children are taught to perform well in tests, partly because they have the general neoliberal mind-set being discussed in this book of the importance of quantitative measures; partly because they want the majority of children to be obedient employees rather than free-thinking individuals; partly because they have been worried by their countries' children's performance in international tests. 'Progressives' on the other hand are likely to stress creativity and the needs of the individual, at the expense of measured performance in acquiring specific bodies of knowledge. Both sides in the debate have called on research evidence, but the outcome rarely hangs on whether one method or another secures better educational performance, because different means of measuring performance are themselves part of the debate. In such cases democracy, influenced by rhetoric and debate, has to determine an overall sense of direction and bias. At that point it passes to professionals to work out the implications, though in such sensitive cases these too will have their prejudices; we can request only that there is no political 'loading' of those involved.

On the other hand it was quite inappropriate when in 2014 the British education minister decided that certain American books should not be on the English literature syllabus of English schools. He consulted an advisory committee of experts before making the intervention, but the issue at hand was far too detailed to be appropriate for political intervention, especially with no prior public debate, and setting a precedent that ministers might dictate what books children might read. The matter should have been pursued entirely through professional channels, excluding political action.

Second, it is right that democratic debate draw attention to general problems of quality and levels of provision in health services. It is doubtful, however, whether it is well placed to decide the relative priorities of different conditions and treatments, as these require highly informed judgement. It has, for example, been noted that for obscure reasons brain tumours do not feature among the cancers that have been the object of public campaigns and fund-raising, though they are just as devastating as many that have benefited from campaigns.

A final example covers both these categories of problems of the inadequacy of democracy. English police forces were given performance targets that emphasized car theft and burglary, as research showed that it was these crimes that determined citizens' perceptions of the level of crime in their area – and therefore reductions in them would add plausibility to governments' claims that they were reducing crime in general. It was this, inter alia, that led to the sexual exploitation of children being ignored by police in several English cities; it was not a crime that was relevant to this perception threshold.

In his book *Hyperdemocracy*, Stephen Welch (2013) criticizes my assertion that we are moving towards 'post-democracy' (Crouch 2004); as his title implies, he considers that we are today insisting on having too much democracy. But he and I are talking about two sides of the same coin rather than taking opposed positions. Democracy, like all institutions of governance, needs a framework set by an authority outside of itself if it is not to undermine itself by using its own powers to change the rules that are supposed to govern it. This is a major reason why the great majority of democratic states have constitutions that can be amended only through very special and difficult procedures rather than simple parliamentary majorities. The UK is a very clear exception here, maintaining the sovereignty of current parliamentary majorities even over constitutional law. This developed from an age when, at least among the small (and not democratic) elite that was then enfranchised, there was widespread if informal understanding over how the rules could be changed. The arrangement has been maintained long since such a situation obtained, raising some doubts over the capacity of the UK to deal with major constitutional change.

In practice democracy needs both formal rules and informal values that are not themselves subject to democratic control, exactly as the market needs external regulation of its parameters as well as what Adam Smith called moral sentiments. In particular these external constraints are needed to restrain powerful interests that have risen within the system and which then use it to make it serve their own interests (powerful political groups in the case of democracy; monopolistic firms in the case of the market). Having achieved control, these groups can use the rhetoric of the system's legitimacy to undermine these external frames, so that they can use the system to extend their own powers further. The emergence of such powerful interests in the polity is part of what I mean by post-democracy, but the consequence of what they do can well be hyper-democracy. When democracy becomes weak, there is a risk that voters will become detached from it. While this leaves the field even more vulnerable to manipulation by powerful interests, these may also become uncomfortable that they lack legitimacy. They need people to vote, and they can increase the chances that they will by politicizing a mass of minor questions; a tactic that also has the advantage of distracting attention from major issues over who is really gaining from the way the system is operating.

Another way of looking at this issue is to say that when political debate is about nothing, it has to be about everything. When there is very little real disagreement among parties over major policy directions (a fundamental characteristic of post-democracy), politicians have to start exploring every little avenue they can in order to claim that they have found a difference from their opponents – anything from each other's personal morality to the desirability of particular medical treatments, numbers of police on the streets, or ways of teaching children to read.

Excessive politicization, or hyper-democracy, is therefore paradoxically an aspect of post-democracy. Similar arguments from an initially completely different perspective have been made by Daniel Zimmer in his book *Weniger Politik!* (2013). His starting position is neoliberal, though, as chair of Germany's Monopoly Commission, he is not the corporate kind of neoliberal that has been mainly criticized here. Also, he acknowledges certain characteristic defects of markets that require regulatory intervention of various kinds: externalities, information asymmetries between producers and customers, monopoly situations, and the existence of public goods. Outside the range of these market failures he argues that politics should not intervene. There is always room for debate over how serious any one of these failures has to be before one seeks political intervention, but the list in itself needs the addition of only one further point to be one that should satisfy most concerns. This is the need, alongside public goods, to protect from the market (and indeed the state) areas of life that a broad consensus of opinion considers should remain private or informal. His argument that, outside specified areas where the market is inadequate, politics should be restrained is a sound one and further helps to establish the boundary between democracy and professional knowledge.

Through such discussions we might achieve some kind of understanding over which kinds of issues are very properly at the heart of passionate political debate, and which are primarily technical questions that should be the domain of professionals. There are no a priori means of making such a distinction, and indeed making it is itself the kind of major decision that is fit meat for democratic controversy. All we can do here is to point to the need for such a debate, to suggest how the lines might be drawn, and (the task that now remains) to indicate the kinds of structures that might best defend the necessary boundaries between democracy and professionalism in the interests of both.

This is not a plea for technocracy: the basic value questions must be addressed and resolved through rhetoric and passionate debate as well as appeals to reason. Geologists must decide whether an oil well is safe, engineers must design bridges, doctors must choose treatments, and care workers must decide how much time they need to devote to the people for whose welfare they are responsible. However, all these activities present opportunity costs. A point is reached where those responsible for funding, whether these are a corporation's owners or a government, ask if this is the best way to spend money. It is probably impossible, except at enormous cost, to guarantee absolutely that an oil well or bridge can withstand any stress to which it might conceivably be subject. Funding of health services would become completely distorted if individual medical practitioners could prescribe medicines completely regardless of the cost. Care workers could well decide that they needed to spend all day with individual patients. Ultimately citizens need to have the democratic capacity to decide how much span should be allowed to private owners in the calculation of risks in producing major negative externalities or damage to collective goods, and to decide the balance of spending among different public services themselves and between them and private spending. At the same time, professionals can be expected to see their tasks in a wider context of priorities if they are given the chance, in discursive groups of colleagues, to shape these within clear guidelines, sharing ownership of the final outcomes.

We must in this context also demand an end to governments trying to 'do good by stealth', that is, addressing causes that seem 'good' but are unpopular. It is a common practice of centre-left governments trying to achieve something for minority groups with serious problems but against help for whom right-wing mass media are likely to agitate: ethnic minorities, immigrants, sufferers from some kinds of mental illness. The whole tenor of my argument in this book is to advocate openness in knowledge. The problem with doing good by stealth is that eventually the actions become objects of public focus, when they then appear as acts of duplicity, while no work has been done to persuade public opinion to take an alternative view of the issue at stake.

Professions in their place

There is then a separate question of the extent to which professionals deserve to be trusted to take responsibility for what they do. This is not just about trust in the sense that they might 'cheat' and claim to be working when they are not, or claim to be using the best knowledge available to them when they have become idle and not bothered to upgrade their skills – though these possibilities do have to be considered and dealt with. More general, and more difficult, is a question of knowledge: of the capacity of users (whether as customers or citizens) to be able to interact with practitioners, and question their judgement, without imposing on them poorly informed practices. In the private sector this is in theory achieved by the market; if we do not like what one practitioner does, we can go to another. However, this does not work in the very many situations where any or all of the classic market failures are present: a small number of large practitioners all doing more or less the same thing, so that there is no choice; massive information asymmetries – the central problem with professional knowledge – so that we are unable to form a competent judgement; the existence of important externalities (as in the Gulf oil disaster), such that it is not only customers who are negatively affected by bad professional practice, but a wide range of others; and where there are collective goods at stake, with a result similar to the problem of externalities. With public services, especially those that have been contracted out, there are further problems in that users have the rights of neither customers nor citizens, but are just objects.

The appropriate response to these issues is not repeated political intervention, but action of two different kinds: inspection and participation.

Inspection   Many of the issues at stake can be fairly successfully tackled through inspection regimes: practitioners who are particularly expert in the field carry out thorough inspections of the work of other professionals and write publicly accessible reports on the quality of that work, having the right to take disciplinary action or even suspend a professional's right to practise when there are major weaknesses. This much-used approach presents some problems. First, carried out properly, it is highly expensive, and removes some of the best professionals from actual practice so that they can become inspectors. These costs simply have to be accepted if we want activities that involve arcane and complex knowledge to be performed properly; just as we accept that motor vehicles should be subject to inspections for road-worthiness and the concomitant costs (and questions can perhaps be raised about the adequacy of such tests). The consequences of not taking this work seriously can be seen in the decline of the English school inspection system, with inspectors not always being of the highest quality and with inspections becoming formulaic, largely tick-box exercises. The sophisticated knowledge-based societies in which we live today have brought us many advantages and a wealth of resources, but unless we are willing to devote a significant share of those resources to maintaining the standards with which knowledge is deployed, we shall be let down and deceived by those wielding that knowledge. Onora O'Neill

(2002) has expressed the basic need in her discussion of the issue of trust in the professions:

> Intelligent accountability, I suspect, requires more attention to good governance and fewer fantasies about total control. Good governance is possible only if institutions are allowed some margin for self-governance of a form appropriate to their particular tasks, within a framework of financial and other reporting. Such reporting, I believe, is not improved by being wholly standardised or relentlessly detailed, and since much that has to be accounted for is not easily measured it cannot be boiled down to a set of stock performance indicators. Those who are called to account should give an account of what they have done and of their successes or failures to others who have sufficient time and experience to assess the evidence and report on it. Real accountability provides substantive and knowledgeable independent judgement of an institution's or professional's work.

A second potential problem is that in their work inspectorates must be free from political and commercial interference and influence. Often these arrangements can be entirely private, unless they come to raise issues of general public importance. A good example is monitoring standards for football referees. At the top level, this is carried out meticulously by football authorities. It can be left in their hands unless there are serious allegations of bribery, in which case the matter becomes one of public interest. Bribery itself is already a criminal offence to be dealt with by police on a case-by-case basis, but were there to be wider concerns about its extent there would probably be demands for some continuing public check on the adequacy of the football authorities' arrangements. When a field of activity is of clear public importance, the appointment of members of inspectorates, supervisory bodies and complaints mechanisms cannot be left entirely to the professionals, as they might conspire to support each other against the public interest. The case for supervisory frameworks of public representatives over inspection regimes results from the fact that, necessarily, expert inspectors come from the same professional group as the one they are inspecting. There are extensive records of professionals covering up for each other, even of the development of an ethic that one does not publicly criticize a colleague even if one knows his work is inadequate. It is for this reason that lay members are often appointed to inspectorates, and these need to have a strong independent relationship to the appointing board responsible for a particular inspection regime. Close to the top of the agenda of their discussions with such boards must always be issues of possible collusion. No system is foolproof, but those involved can at least be required to be alert. Questions of cover-up, political bias and improper commercial interests have to be discussed candidly and seriously, not relegated to tick-box exercises or the application of purely formal criteria. For example, it occasionally happens that a person charged over a matter of commercial corruption will settle the case out of court, in order to avoid incurring a conviction that might disqualify her from holding various offices in corporations. Willingness to settle out of court with payment of a large sum of money should be taken as prima facie evidence that the person concerned is of questionable integrity and not fit to hold the offices in question.

Since there is always a risk of either regulatory capture by those being regulated, or political interference on behalf of favourites or to help the government of the day, appointment of independent members of these bodies must be like those for arm's-length public bodies discussed earlier: in the hands of multi-partite bodies, not governments of the day by themselves. Also, the doctrine of NPM that public officials will benefit from having extensive contacts with the private sector must be set aside for these activities. The need for complete avoidance of corruption and improper influence has to trump the gains that might come from commercial or political involvement. Use has to be made of secondments and similar contacts at other, less sensitive, parts of the system. There has to be maximum transparency, and substantive rather than formal rules established and obeyed. (It is not, for example, adequate for someone to claim to have no longer any interest at stake because he has sold his shares to his wife.)

Professions and public participation   Participation, or two-sided communication between professionals and their users, is both easier and more difficult to arrange. It is simpler because it does not involve the establishment of elaborate and costly systems as with inspection regimes; it is more complex because it involves very large numbers of people and has to confront the gulf in expertise and knowledge that divides professionals from users of their services. The neo-liberal market model tries to resolve the problem in its characteristic way: the professional offers a service; if the customer/client finds it unsatisfactory, she goes elsewhere. Poor-quality practitioners are therefore driven from the market. If customers/clients feel that the information asymmetries between them and the professionals are too severe to enable them to make choices, there will be a market for informed customer advice services, which people will choose to use. (Neoliberals might also use this argument about a market for advice services as an argument for there not being a need for inspection regimes for professional services located in the private sector.)

The problem with this approach is that discussed in chapter 2 in connection with ratings agencies. Customers face the same difficulty of information asymmetry when they use advice services as they do with professionals themselves: how do we know we can trust an advice service when we cannot understand the knowledge on which it bases its advice? The neoliberal response is of course again to trust the market: advice services that are unsatisfactory will be driven out as customers experience poor service. But that can work only if there is a true market in such services, that is, a large number of providers. But the larger the number of these, the more difficult is it for reputation (the only form of knowledge that enables non-expert customers to choose providers) to spread. This has become a problem with the proliferation of price comparison websites designed to help customers choose providers in complex markets such as domestic energy. As with ratings agencies, services of this kind usually charge the firms or other organizations being rated rather than the customers; if the latter were to be charged there is nothing to stop them sharing information with others, and the market would collapse. But if the firms being rated pay for the service there is always a suspicion that they will pay commission to comparison websites if these can attract customers to them. Achieving this commission then becomes the profit-maximizing route for the website, not the provision of reliable advice to customers.

As we have seen at several points, in public services, including in particular those that are contracted out to private providers, the user is not even a customer, and is in severe danger of becoming just an object of a service. Here the dignity of citizenship provides a more appropriate model for placing the relationship between professionals and users on a good footing than the false analogy of customer status. To be a citizen implies a right to be treated with respect, to be able to engage in genuinely interactive communication, to be helped to understand where knowledge asymmetries make interaction difficult. The entire trend of public-service reform has been against this concept, and to move instead to treatment of service users as pseudo-customers. But, as we have repeatedly shown, the rights of customers consist only in the capacity to go elsewhere, which implies a market of many producers that is often absent. In the case of out-sourced public services where a public authority is the customer, the user has none of the rights of a customer at all. We also have massive evidence from advertising and market research in all sectors of the private economy that the competitive market gives few incentives to firms to overcome the information asymmetries between themselves and their customers. Instead they boast, distort, and in particular replace the transmission of actual information with the association of their brand with favourable emotional imagery. There are exceptions where customers are other firms, with their own professionals engaged in making purchases, or in small, high-cost, elite ends of markets where individual customers are likely to be well informed, and to have a personal relationship with producers. This is not the experience of the vast majority of people making everyday purchases.

What happens when public services adopt a strong customer approach to their users can be well illustrated by the case of British universities. These have long been engaged in a well-functioning market relationship with applicants for admission as students: people hoping to attend university could apply to up to six different institutions; university departments would then make offers of places to the applicants they wanted. Both sides made choices; both were motivated to get the best they could. Both sides provided information: applicants in their lists of school successes and other biographical details; universities in details about their courses. An implicit culture of restraint limited the way in which information was transmitted by both sides. In recent years, as universities have been given financial incentives by government to recruit as many students as possible, the nature of these communications from universities has changed. Where they previously issued highly factual, somewhat boringly presented, information, they now set out to sell themselves. They boast, lay claims to excellence that might well be unfounded, surround their increasingly less informative factual texts with pictures and words conveying what a wonderful life students will enjoy, without any necessary basis in fact.

Similar changes occur as other public services are actually privatized or where public providers have to pretend that they are in markets. The consequence is a massive proliferation of words and images that do nothing to tackle the true problems of information asymmetry but in contrast add to information overload by boasting, making unsupported claims and trying at an emotional level of communication to provide favourable associations for their brand. Police cars, rubbish collection vehicles, dentists' waiting rooms all join this growth of meaningless and unhelpful verbiage by carrying empty aspirational slogans on their vehicles and walls. Meanwhile users are left none the wiser and perhaps even more confused than before about what is actually happening to them. The status of customer, especially where it lacks the attributes of the true, up-market customer, is considerably inferior to that of citizen.

Always, but especially in those cases where users are not true customers, professionals have to learn how to treat them as citizens, sharing information with them, listening, and trying to break down the mystique that often surrounds their admittedly special and important knowledge. To advocate this is not utopian; it already happens in large numbers of cases. The attack on professions as uniformly arrogant, inaccessible and both unable and unwilling to break down the mysteries surrounding their knowledge is partly politically motivated. Politicians wanting to privatize a service, or submit it to primarily financial incentives, find it convenient to encourage that stereotype and make public-service professions unpopular. For example, authorities are usually very hostile to 'whistle-blowers', employees who reveal cases of wrongdoing or bad practice that their superiors are trying to conceal. Suddenly, in 2013 the UK government made an exception of the NHS, where it issued a charter for the protection of whistle-blowers. This coincided with a period when the government was seeking popular support for the privatization of service delivery right across the NHS, a service that enjoyed strong public support and suspicion against privatization. Mass media journalists whose own profession has degraded its standards so heavily in the face of commercial pressures are happy to assist with the task of undermining professional reputations.

There are of course arrogant, remote professionals; but there are many who are not. Younger generations of teachers, medical practitioners, lawyers and others have developed far more approachable, interactive styles of communication. Confident in their professional knowledge, which is usually more securely grounded than that of earlier times, they do not need to hide it behind a mystical screen, but are happy to share with parents, patients and other types of client. The feminization of most of these professions has considerably assisted this process, as (to risk a broad generalization) the early socialization of girls in most cultures tends to enable women to be more at ease in informal and two-sided interaction than their more task-focused male colleagues. The practices and approaches of professionals (men and women alike) who have developed these communicative skills can be studied and understood by their own professional bodies and by government agencies, incorporated into training and retraining programmes, and built into the issues that inspectors consider when visiting services. A good deal of such work has indeed been done, in many countries and services. More could have been achieved had public-service reform not engaged in the wild goose chase of turning every service user into an artificial form of customer rather than exploring what would be needed to make them true citizens of the welfare state.

A major problem for such reforms is the difficulty of ensuring equality of citizenship status for people with very diverse levels of education, income and social prestige. Here too the customer model is of little help, as it is fundamental to the concept of the customer that the richer one is the better the treatment one receives. The customer analogy can be of some value, where users have a chance of informed choice; schools worried that a decline in numbers of parents choosing them could lead to their closure will make efforts to do well. But it will not help where there is no choice or where users are of low status. The examples discussed in the previous chapter of the treatment by British private providers of care in children's services and for elderly and disabled people demonstrate that clearly. They also showed how the carers responsible for such disregarded groups are themselves being deprofessionalized and deskilled.

There is no automatic solution to these issues in public service. With the best will in the world, medical practitioners will find it easier and more satisfying to discuss patients' illnesses when patients are articulate, well educated and from a similar social milieu to themselves. Few school teachers find it easy to communicate with parents who have little knowledge of education and perhaps come from a different cultural background. Whether in these issues, or in participation in democracy, or in treatment by law courts, the formal equality proclaimed by the idea of citizenship is very difficult to guarantee in practice. Such issues can, however, be less well or better addressed. And it is legitimate for democratic institutions to debate the relative priority to be given such questions, even if it is unwise for them to become too involved in thinking up practical solutions.

Conclusions

No utopia is available to us of a world where knowledge is never manipulated or distorted by those with the power to do so. Our ability to act as competent customers and citizens in complex situations will always be weakened by information asymmetries. We cannot avoid dependence on markets that give suppliers incentives to ignore important information or to deceive us, or on professionals who do not merit the trust that we have to place in them, or on politicians who seize on and exaggerate these problems in order to enhance their own positions. But we are also not helpless. Regulation, inspection and the enforcement of professional codes all have good records of helping us confront these problems. The main danger we face today is that the ruling model of neoliberalism claims to have found, in the market, the most effective answer to them, while it also provides many incentives for producers and providers to manipulate and distort. In this context it is urgent to recognize not just the continuing but the enhanced need for those other, non-market means of protecting us.

The most positive finding in preceding chapters has been that, despite the outsourcings, the search for economies in service provision in the interests of profit-maximizing private equity firms owning social policy delivery, and a denigration of professionals, there have been no moves in the UK to deskill the labour forces involved in teaching and health services. Indeed, the opposite has taken place. This has happened, not because a customer model of these services has triumphed, but because democratic political debate has prioritized them. If there are constant attempts to improve the schools and health care in that country, it is because British people are still citizens of a welfare state, and their concerns for these services require governments to respond. Sadly, the truth of this observation can best be demonstrated by looking at what has befallen services for groups who lack democratic power: young girls in care, the elderly in care, the mentally ill. No private equity firm has moved schools to areas where land is cheaper, or imposed rents on hospitals whose land they own so high that they have to employ poor-quality staff, though they have done all these things to parentless children and the very old. The outcry from citizens with the vote would be too great.

This situation may change. Some hospitals are indeed in financial difficulties because they entered into private finance initiatives that secured private capital for building programmes at the expense of long, expensive pay-back requirements. Private finance initiatives were a favourite NPM device of the 1997–2010 UK Labour governments, but they have since become discredited for the costs and rigidities they impose. At present, greater risks to citizen power in the British welfare state come from the rise of private health insurance as people try to queue-jump the crowded public service, and the disintegration of the school system as corporations make private, confidential contracts with government to run groups of schools outside the range of the legislation governing the national system. If eventually users of the NHS and normal state schools no longer represent majorities, these institutions may go the way of child- and elderly care services. In the meantime, however, the citizenship model has shown its continuing strength.

The most depressing finding in these chapters has been the evidence of crises of trust that they have presented. The world's leading banks and other leading corporations have been involved in some outrageously dishonest behaviour; professions have distorted the priorities of their duties by gaming targets; NPM has legitimated a mass of dubious interactions among politicians, officials and private contractors. Economic theory gives us two alternative approaches to trust. Some theorists would argue that it saves on transaction costs, as the mechanisms of monitoring and control that have to operate where trust is low are costly. Others are more sceptical: trust cannot be calculated; it can lead to inefficiency where a practitioner's record of trustworthiness prevents us from market-testing against alternatives; it is vulnerable to exploitation by those who use our trust to betray it. Ideally, therefore, we should exercise trust up until the point where the savings it brings in transitional costs are outweighed by the costs of inefficiency and potential betrayal. The problem with that advice is that it is impossible to take it when there are major knowledge asymmetries between us and those we are contemplating trusting – the situation with which this book has been concerned.

Inspection regimes can be seen as means of matching the costs of trust and mistrust in a way that the market itself cannot achieve because of these asymmetries. The need for inspection is of course an expression of our lack of trust, and its costs are the costs of that lack. But an inspection regime can discover that some practitioners deserve more trust than others (whether because of their honesty or because of their competence). These can be inspected more lightly: that is trust reducing the costs of monitoring.

The alternative lesson to which economic reasoning leads us in these situations is not to risk trust, but to use the market: do not trust providers, but set up incentives that reward them if they behave well and punish them if they behave badly. But this can become involved in a vicious spiral between loss of trust and measures to compensate for it. It is difficult to tell where any given spiral might start, but let us assume that loss of trust has occurred in a professional group. We therefore give them targets against which they must perform, their incomes being based on their performance. Pursuit of a professional ethic is replaced by working to targets, which leads to gaming of targets, which implies a further decline of trustworthiness. Continuing down the road of setting ever tighter performance incentives only exacerbates the process. Eventually one arrives at the position reached by the US courts trying to cope with serious criminal behaviour in the financial sector. Banks' key staffs continue to be offered the chances of astronomical salaries and bonuses, which provide an extraordinary temptation to dishonesty; the courts respond with ever higher fines. It is possible that these fines will simply be passed on to customers, but if they really do bite into banks' profits, should banks respond by changing the material incentive structure so that somehow it rewards only honest behaviour, or by trying to develop some idea of ethical standards, which staff do not overstep? The former approach resigns itself to accepting amoral profit maximization, and hopes to keep one step ahead of the discovery of new tricks by very smart operators; the latter is always vulnerable to exploitation of a trust that has been regained.

So many of us in a society where great rewards are to be had by a few have eaten of the tree of knowledge of good and evil and found that the latter pays. Is it ever possible to tread the path back from that situation? Are we willing to accept the costs of inspection regimes that would help us to do so?

References

Chapter 1   Neoliberalism and the Problem of Knowledge

Becker, G. 1960. *A Treatise on the Family*. Cambridge MA: Harvard University Press.

Becker, G. 1964. *Human Capital*. Chicago IL: Chicago University Press.

BMJ. 2014. An open letter to Simon Stevens, NHS chief executive, and Alistair Burns, national clinical lead for dementia. *BMJ*, 6 November, 349.

Crouch, C. 2004. *Post-Democracy*. Cambridge: Polity.

Foucault, M. 2004. *Naissance de la biopolitique*. Paris: Gallimard-Seuil.

Hayek, F. A. von. 1944. *The Road to Serfdom*. London: Routledge.

Hayek, F. A. von. 1948. *Individualism and Economic Order*. London: Routledge.

Hayek, F. A. von. 1960. *The Constitution of Liberty*. Chicago IL: Chicago University Press.

Jensen, M. 2001. Value maximization, stakeholder theory, and the corporate objective function. *Journal of Applied Corporate Finance*, 14, 3: 8–21.

Marcuse, H. 1964. *One-Dimensional Man*. London: Routledge.

Mirowski, P. 2013. *Never Let a Good Crisis Go to Waste: How Neoliberalism Survived the Financial Meltdown*. London: Verso.

O'Neill, O. 2002. *A Question of Trust: The BBC Reith Lectures 2002.* http://www.bbc.co.uk/radio4/features/the-reith-lectures/transcripts/2000/#y2002 (Later published as *A Question of Trust.* Cambridge: Cambridge University Press.)

Piketty, T. 2013. *Le capital au 21e siècle.* Paris: Éditions du Seuil.

Thaler, R. H. and Sunstein, C. R. 2008. *Nudge: Improving Decisions about Health, Wealth, and Happiness.* New Haven CT: Yale University Press.

Chapter 2 Knowledge and the Problem of Capitalism

Aldrick, P. 2013. PPI compensation spurs economy through spending boost. *Telegraph,* 17 August.

Aspen Institute. 2009. *Overcoming Short-Termism: A Call for a More Responsible Approach to Investment and Business Management.* Washington DC: Aspen Institute.

BBC. 2013. BBC 2 series *Bankers,* May.

Broder, J. M. 2010. Panel says firms knew of cement flaws before spill. *New York Times,* 28 October.

Brummer, A. 2014. *Bad Banks: Greed, Incompetence and the Next Global Crisis.* London: Business Books.

Calkins, L. B. 2011. US in contempt over Gulf drill ban, judge rules. *Bloomberg,* 3 February.

Cantuar. 2013. LISTEN: Archbishop Justin on good banks. http://www.archbishopofcanterbury.org/articles.php/5075/listen-archbishop-justin-on-good-banks

Chivers, T. 2014. The Tamiflu scandal will be repeated, and people will die, unless drug companies release all their data. *Telegraph,* 11 April.

Crouch, C. 2015. *Governing Social Risks in Post-Crisis Europe.* Cheltenham: Elgar.

Davies, N. 2009. Revealed: Murdoch's £1m bill for hiding dirty tricks. *Guardian,* 9 July.

Davies, N. 2014. *Hack Attack.* London: Chatto and Windus.

Deakin, N. and Rogowski, R. 2011. Reflexive labour law, capabilities and the future of social Europe. In Rogowski, R., Salais, R. and Whiteside, N. (eds.) *Transforming European Employment Policy: Labour Market Transitions and the Promotion of Capability.* Cheltenham: Elgar, 229–54.

Dunlap, R. E. and McCright, A. M. 2012. Organized climate change denial: sources, actors and strategies. In Lever-Troby, C. (ed.) *Routledge Handbook of Climate Change and Society*. London: Routledge, 240–59.

Erturk, I., Froud, J., Johal, S. and Williams, K. 2004. Corporate governance and disappointment. *Review of International Political Economy*, 11, 4: 677–713.

Financial Conduct Authority. 2015. Deutsche Bank fined £227 million .... http://www.fca.org.uk/news/deutsche-bank-fined-by-fca-for-libor-and-euribor-failings

FSA. 2012. Final Notice, Barclays Bank Plc, 27 June.

Goldacre, B. 2012. *Bad Pharma*. London: Fourth Estate.

Goldacre, B. 2014. It's a scandal drug trial results are still being withheld. *Guardian*, 5 January.

Goldenberg, S. 2011. Emails expose BP's attempts to control research into impact of Gulf oil spill. *Guardian*, 15 April.

Government of Greece. 2012. *Memorandum of Understanding on Specific Economic Policy Conditionality, 9 February 2012*. Athens: Government of Greece.

Guthrie, J. 2014. Regulators slap $4.3bn fines on six banks in global Forex scandal. *Financial Times*, 12 November.

Hmielowski, J. D., Feldman, L., Myers, T. A., Leiserowitz, A. and Maibach, E. 2014. An attack on science? Media use, trust in scientists, and perceptions of global warming. *Public Understanding of Science*, 23, 7: 866–83.

Höpner, M. 2008. Usurpation statt Delegation. MPIfG Discussion Paper 08/12. Cologne: Max Planck Institute for the Study of Societies.

House of Commons. 2012. *An Inquiry into the Culture, Practices and Ethics of the Press*. House of Commons Paper HC 779. London: HMSO.

Laverty, A. A., Dietheim, P., Hopkinson, N. S., Watt, H. C. and McKee, M. 2014. Use and abuse of statistics in tobacco industry-funded research on standardized packaging. *Tobacco Control*, doi:10.1136/tobaccocontrol-2014-052051

Lexchin, J., Bero, L. A., Djulbegovic, B. and Clark, O. 2003. Pharmaceutical industry sponsorship, research outcome and quality: a systematic review. *BMJ*, 326, 7400: 1167.

Mazur, R. 2013. How to halt the terrorist money train. *New York Times*, 2 January.

Miller, D. and Harkins, C. 2010. Corporate strategy, corporate capture: food and alcohol industry lobbying and public health. *Critical Social Policy*, 30, 4: 564–89.

National Diet of Japan. 2012. *Official Report of the Fukushima Nuclear Accident Independent Investigation Commission.* Tokyo: National Diet of Japan.

O'Neill, O. 2002. *A Question of Trust: The BBC Reith Lectures 2002.* http://www.bbc.co.uk/radio4/features/the-reith-lectures/transcripts/2000/#y2002 (Later published as *A Question of Trust.* Cambridge: Cambridge University Press.)

Osborne, H. 2012. PPI exposé: how the banks drove staff to mis-sell the insurance. *Guardian*, 8 November.

Rai, S. 2001. India-US fight on basmati rice is mostly settled. *New York Times*, 25 August.

Rankin, J. 2014. Lloyds bill for missold PPI rises to £11 bn. *Guardian*, 28 October.

Sol, C. C. A. M. and Van der Vos, M. R. 2013. *SGEI: The Case of Social Housing in the Netherlands.* European Union FP7 project GUSTO. http://www.gusto-project.eu/index.php?option=com_content&view=article&id=336:paper&catid=44:wp5&Itemid=61

Treanor, J. 2015. Deutsche Bank hit by record $2.5bn Libor-rigging fine. *Guardian*, 23 April.

Urbina, I. 2010a. US said to allow drilling without needed permits. *New York Times*, 13 May.

Urbina, I. 2010b. Documents show early worries about safety of rig. *New York Times*, 29 May.

USCSHIB. 2005. *Investigation Report: Refinery Explosion and Fire.* Washington DC: USCSHIB.

US Supreme Court. 2013. *Organic Seed Growers and Trade Association, et al., v. Monsanto Company, et al.* Supreme Court Case No. 13-303. Washington DC: US Supreme Court.

Washburn, S. 2007. Science's worst enemy: corporate funding. *Discover*, 11 October.

Webb, T. 2010. WikiLeaks cables: BP suffered blowout on Azerbaijan gas platform. *Guardian*, 16 December.

Chapter 3   The Corrosion of the Public-Service Ethos

Bingham, J. 2012. NHS millions for controversial care pathway. *Telegraph*, 31 October.

Chang, H.-J. 2007. *Bad Samaritans*. London: Random House.

Collier, P. M. 2006. In search of purpose and priorities: police performance indicators in England and Wales. *Money and Management*, 26, 3.

Crouch, C. 2011. *The Strange Non-Death of Neoliberalism*. Cambridge: Polity.

Davies, G. 2014. Council asks academy chains to explain Croydon's 'disappearing' pupils. *Croydon Advertiser*, 13 February.

Dodd, V. 2013. Rape victim 'pressured by police to drop claim against man who later killed'. *Guardian*, 26 February.

Donnelly, L. and Sawer, P. 2013. 13,000 died needlessly at 14 worst NHS trusts. *Telegraph*, 13 July.

Edwards, N. 2015. The way the NHS manages A&E problems is not fit for purpose. *Health Service Journal*, 2 March.

Foley, B. and Goldstein, H. 2012. *League Tables in the Public Sector*. London: British Academy.

Goldstein, H. and Myers, K. 1996. Freedom of information: towards a code of ethics for performance indicators. *Research Intelligence*, 57: 12–16.

Halliday, J. 2014. South Yorkshire police face new criticism over handling of major crime. *Guardian*, 28 August.

HMIC. 2013. *South Yorkshire Police: Response to Child Sexual Exploitation*. London: HMIC.

Hood, C. 1991. A public management for all seasons. *Public Administration*, 69: 3–19.

IPCC. 2013. *Southwark Sapphire Unit's Local Practices for the Reporting and Investigation of Sexual Offences, July 2008– September 2009*. London: IPCC.

Keogh, B. 2013. *Review into the Quality of Care and Treatment Provided by 14 Hospital Trusts in England: Overview Report*. London: NHS.

Le Grand, J. 2006. *Motivation, Agency and Public Policy: Of Knights and Knaves, Pawns and Queens*. Revised paperback edn. Oxford: Oxford University Press.

Mansell, W. 2014. The strange case of the vanishing GCSE pupils. *Guardian*, 21 January.

Neuberger, Lady. 2013. *More Care, Less Pathway: Review of Liverpool Care Pathway for Dying Patients*. London: HMSO.

Neville, S. 2013. Schools found to be stacking up exam entries to hit targets. *Financial Times*, 1 August.

NHS England. 2012. News analysis: what is the Liverpool Care Pathway?   http://www.nhs.uk/news/2012/11November/Pages/What-is-the-Liverpool-Care-Pathway.aspx

OECD. 2003. *Managing Decentralization: A New Role for Labour Market Policy.* Paris: OECD.

O'Neill, O. 2002. *A Question of Trust: The BBC Reith Lectures 2002.* http://www.bbc.co.uk/radio4/features/the-reith-lectures/transcripts/2000/#y2002 (Later published as *A Question of Trust.* Cambridge: Cambridge University Press.)

Osborne, D. and Gaebler, T. 1993. *Reinventing Government: How the Entrepreneurial Spirit is Transforming the Public Sector.* Reading MA: Addison-Wesley.

Piketty, T. 2013. *Le capital au 21e siècle.* Paris: Éditions du Seuil.

Schekman, R. 2013. How journals like Nature, Cell and Science are damaging science. *Guardian*, 9 December.

Spottiswoode, C. 2000. *Improving Police Performance.* Public Services Productivity Panel. London: HMSO.

UK Government. 1963. *Higher Education*, Cmnd 2154. London: HMSO.

UK Government. 2010. *Independent Review of Higher Education Funding and Student Finance.* London: HMSO.

Chapter 4   Knowledge for Citizens, Customers or Objects?

Baxter, J. 2014. An independent inspectorate? Addressing the paradoxes of educational inspection. *School Leadership and Management*, 34, 1: 21–38.

BBC. 2011. Revolving Doors. Radio 4 programme. *File on Four*, 26 July.

BMJ. 2013. BMJ investigation finds GP conflicts of interest 'rife' on commissioning boards. *BMJ*, 12 March.

Booth, R. and Hopkins, N. 2012. Olympic security chaos: depth of G4S security crisis revealed. *Guardian*, 13 July.

Bronner, E. 2012. Poor land in jail as companies add huge fees for probation. *New York Times*, 2 July.

Chakrabortty, A. 2014. Outsourced and unaccountable: this is the future of local government. *Guardian*, 15 December.

Cridland, J. 2013. CBI chief warns against demonization of outsourcing groups. *Financial Times*, 19 November.

Davis, J., Lister, J. and Wrigley, D. 2015. *NHS for Sale: Myths, Lies and Deception*. London: Merlin.

Exley, S. 2012. Inspectors unqualified to teach sit in judgement. *Times Education Supplement*, 27 July.

Lawrence, F. 2013. Private contractor fiddled data when reporting to NHS, says watchdog. *Guardian*, 7 March.

Le Grand, J. 2006. *Motivation, Agency and Public Policy: Of Knights and Knaves, Pawns and Queens*. Revised paperback edn. Oxford: Oxford University Press.

Leigh, D., Ball, J., Garside, J. and Pegg, D. 2015. HSBC files show how Swiss bank helped clients dodge taxes and hide millions. *Guardian*, 8 February.

London Borough of Barnet. 2009. *Future Shape*. Barnet: London Borough of Barnet.

Mason, R. and Campbell, D. 2014. Civil service chief under fire for keeping job at drink manufacturer. *Guardian*, 29 October.

Morris, N. and Pells, R. 2014. Serco given Yarl's Wood immigration contract despite 'vast failings'. *Independent*, 24 November.

Neville, S. 2011. £1 bn gamble of the care home sharks revealed: Southern Cross predators sold off almost 300 homes to RBS. *Daily Mail*, 4 June.

Observer. 2014. Editorial. *Observer*, 9 August.

Osborne, A. 2014. G4S wins first central government contract since tagging scandal. *Telegraph*, 15 April.

Parry, S. 2010. Britain's top tax official enjoys £6,000 four-night stay at a luxury hotel in India...to make a 30-MINUTE speech. *Daily Mail*, 12 December.

Paterson, O. 2014. I'm proud of standing up to the green lobby. *Telegraph*, 20 July.

Plimmer, G. 2014. Private groups invited to help NHS buy services. *Financial Times*, 25 February.

Policy Exchange. 2014. *Privatising Justice: Myths, Threats, Opportunities*. London: Policy Exchange.

Quinn, B. 2015. Dozens of arms firm employees on MoD secondments. *Guardian*, 16 February.

Ramesh, R. 2014. Spending breakdown reveals how NHS England cash flowed to private firms. *Guardian*, 27 November.

Reuters. 2012. Talisman fined for 2011 fracking spill. Reuters 4 January.

Ruddick, G. 2009. Meet Serco, the company running the country. *Telegraph*, 26 August.

Sewell, D. 2009. *The Political Gene*. London: Picador.

Sewell, D. 2010. Michael Gove vs the Blob. *Spectator*, 13 January.

Smith, O. 2013. Ryanair 'worst' brand for customer service. *Telegraph*, 19 September.

Social Enterprise UK. 2012. *The Shadow State*. London: Social Enterprise UK.

Tadeo, M. 2013. G4S and Serco lose tagging contracts after overcharging scandal. *Independent*, 12 December.

Taylor, M. 2014. Companies with links to Tories 'have won £1.5 bn worth of NHS contracts'. *Guardian*, 2 October.

Telegraph. 2014. Stephen Dorrell MP faces calls to resign over conflict of interest. *Telegraph*, 1 December.

Townsend, M. 2014. Serco, the Observer, and a hunt for the truth about Yarl's Wood asylum centre. *Guardian*, 17 May.

TUC. 2014. *Education Not for Sale*. London: TUC.

Tuck, P. 2013. The changing role of tax governance: remaking the large corporate taxpayer into a visible customer partner. *British Journal of Management*, 24, Issue Supplement S1: 116–31.

UK Parliament. 2011. *Report of House of Commons Public Accounts Committee: HMRC 2010–11 Accounts: Tax Disputes*. London: HMSO.

UK Parliament. 2013. *Report: Out of Hours GP Services in Cornwall*. House of Commons Public Accounts Committee, 11 July. London: HMSO.

Watt, H. and Prince, R. 2010. Andrew Lansley bankrolled by private healthcare provider. *Telegraph*, 14 January.

West Sussex Adults Safeguarding Board. 2014. *Orchid House: Serious Case Review*. Brighton: West Sussex County Council.

Chapter 5 Citizens, Customers, Politicians, Professionals and Moneymen

Crouch, C. 2004. *Post-Democracy*. Cambridge: Polity.

Hirschman, A. O. 1970. *Exit, Voice and Loyalty*. Cambridge MA: Harvard University Press.

O'Neill, O. 2002. *A Question of Trust: The BBC Reith Lectures 2002*. http://www.bbc.co.uk/radio4/features/the-reith-lectures/transcripts/2000/#y2002 (Later published as *A Question of Trust*. Cambridge: Cambridge University Press.)

Seaton, J. 2008. *Power without Responsibility: Press, Broadcasting and the Internet in Britain.* 7th edn. London: Routledge.
Welch, S. 2013. *Hyperdemocracy.* Basingstoke: Palgrave Macmillan.
Zimmer, D. 2013. *Weniger Politik! Plädoyer für eine freiheitso-rientierte Konzeption von Staat und Rech.* Munich: C. H. Beck.

Index

airlines sector 117, 120, 121–2
Aspen Institute, Colorado 39
Avandia 55

Bank of England 46
banks *see* financial sector
Barclays 45
Barclays Cycle Hire Scheme 103
basmati rice 61–2
Baxter, Jacqueline 112
Bayer CropScience 61
Bayh-Doles Act (1980) 56
BBC (British Broadcasting Corporation) 98
Becker, Gary 27–8
Belfield, Gary 106, 108
Bennett, William 97
The Blob (film, 1958) 97–8
Bridgepoint Capital, European Advisory Panel of 106
British Academy report (2012) 75, 80, 82
British Behavioural Insights Team ('Nudge Unit') 8

British Medical Journal (BMJ) 1, 54–5, 107
British Petroleum (BP) 32, 36–8, 48, 53, 63, 107, 130, 139
Britnell, Mark 106, 108
Browne, Lord 37, 86
Browne Report (2010) 86–7
Brummer, Alex 48
BSkyB 141
BT 105
Business Link 103

Cameron, David 98
Capita 101, 109, 122
Care Quality Commission (CQC) 103, 114–15
Care UK 106, 115
CfBT 77, 112
Cheney, Richard 36
childcare service 113–14, 130, 131, 157
Citigroup 46
citizen rights 123, 124–5, 134–5

citizen-customers 100
  conflictual partners 137
  and firms 137–40
  and political
    decision-makers 140–9
  and professionals 149–58
  status of 156, 157
  see also customers
civil service 107
Cleveland Clinic (Cleveland,
    Ohio) 55
climate change 53, 98
Cochrane Library 54
Condon, Lord 105
Confederation of British
    Industry (CBI) 109
consumer sovereignty 27
corporate sector
  amorality of 64–5
  control of sponsorship of
    research 53–6
  corruption in 24–6
  financial incentives 44–5
  governance in 38–9
  government contractors
    103–4
  information
    asymmetries 154–5
  and innovation 39–40
  lobbying power 25, 43–4,
    59, 63, 64, 107, 123,
    138
  and monopoly rights 62
  political involvement 63–4
  relationship with customers/
    citizens 137–40
  and reputation 139–40
  and short-term vs long-term
    considerations 39–40
  spreading false
    knowledge 35–7

value of firm 35
withholding information
    from customers 42–4
credit cards 22–3
Cridland, John 109
customers
  advice services for
    153–4
  citizen rights 123, 124–5
  exit/voice 136
  nudging technique 124–5
  prisoners as 116
  pseudo-customers 119, 126,
    127, 154
  queue jumping 123
  rail travellers 116–17
  and rational choice
    calculations 133–5
  relationship with firms
    137–40
  rich/poor distinction 118–
    19, 123–4, 127
  status of 156
  students as 117
  taxpayers as 117–19
  as users or objects 100, 116,
    126, 127, 129, 135–7,
    136–7, 154
  see also citizen-customers

Daily Mail (newspaper) 48,
    94, 119
Daily Telegraph (newspaper)
    81–2, 94–5, 104
Dalton, Ian 105, 108
Darwin, Charles 98
Davies, Nick 50, 51
Deepwater Horizon 32, 36,
    37
dementia incentive
    payments 1–2, 10, 72

democracy 4, 24, 30, 158, 159
  boundary with professional knowledge 147
  citizen preferences 143–4
  and citizenship 140
  in education 144–5
  formal rules/informal values 146–7
  in health provision 145
  hyper-democracy 146–7
  inadequacy of 145
  move towards post-democracy 145–6
  and openness in knowledge 149
  protected from politics 143
  rhetoric, debate, appeals to reason 148–9
Diamond, Bob 45
Docklands Light Railway 103
Dorrell, Stephen 106
Dutch social housing 62

easyJet 120
education
  and concept of the Blob 97–8
  contracting out of schools 102
  game targets 77–8, 131
  government commissions 89–90
  government involvement 72
  government reviews 85–6
  improvement in 159
  increase in number of universities 90
  league tables 80–1, 92–3
  legislative reforms 91
  linked to earnings potential 7–8, 26, 85–8, 117
  market analogue approach 110, 129
  outsourcing 100
  parental communication 158
  performance indicators 74, 75–6, 94, 129
  political interventions 145
  progressive 144–5
  school inspections 110–13, 130, 150
  undermining of skill base 113
  university recruitment 155
  use of assistants 125
  use of nudge technique in 28, 87
  see also university research
elderly care 114–15, 130, 131, 157
energy industry 53
ethics
  British press 50–1, 69–70, 132
  corporate 64
  financial sector 82
  and information 19
  and knowledge 2–3, 5–6, 65
  Le Grand's approach 71–3
  professional 68–9, 72, 82, 88, 94, 99, 127, 129, 152, 161
  public service 68, 72, 92, 94–6
  in welfare state 131
Euribor 45–6
Euroland debtor countries 40–2, 89, 130

European Central Bank (ECB) 40–1
European Council of Ministers 43
European Court 62
European Parliament 43
European Union (EU) 40–2, 43–4, 61, 89, 106

Falciani, Hervé 118
Federal Education Act (2001) 81
financial crisis (2007–08) 49, 92
  austerity/deregulation 40–2
  corruption/dishonesty 20–1
  forms of information 16–17
  and problem of speed 89
  reputational damage 21
  role of trust 21–3
  trigger process 16
financial expertise
  concluding remarks 62–5
  conflict with other expertise 35–42
  control over generation/ dissemination of knowledge 53–6
  incentive to distort/corrupt knowledge 44–53
  incentive to withhold information from customers 42–4
  and privatization of public good of knowledge 56–62
  as privileged form of knowledge 34
  and suppression of knowledge 32–3, 34–5

financial sector
  amorality in 64
  banking scandals 45–6
  dominance of money 1–2
  ethics in 94, 161
  misselling of PPI 47–8
  money laundering 48
  possibility of future crises 48–9
  reputation of 48
  rigging of currency exchange system 46–7, 131
  speed of action 89, 129–30
  trust/honesty in 49, 94, 159–60
  use of indicators in 93–4
Fitch's 20
food labelling 43–4
Forex 46–7
Foucault, Michel 26
Fox network 53, 141
fracking 107
Freer, Mike 119
Fukushima nuclear power plant 33, 38, 130

G4S 101, 105, 108–10
Gaebler, Ted 67
gaming technique 76–7, 131, 160
  in education 77–8
  in police force 80
  in university research 78–80
genetically modified organisms (GMOs) 59–61, 132
German Deutsche Bank 46
Germanwings 121
GlaxoSmithKline 54, 55
Goldacre, Ben 54, 55

Goldman Sachs 46, 48, 119
Gove, Michael 97
government sector
  and choosing public-service
    providers 6
  citizen expectations 143–4
  control of 25
  and democracy 142–9
  and doing good by stealth
    149
  and expressions of
    preferences 11
  and financial knowledge 35
  financial sector involvement
    48
  and human capital 28
  involvement in public
    services 73
  making value choices 143
  political power/
    representation 142–3
  provision of information
    140–1
  response to citizens'
    demands 140–1
  setting up of institutions
    142, 143
  and trust 9–10, 14, 24
  and undermining of
    professionals 30
  use of indicators/
    performance scores 4,
    7–10
  use of nudge technique 8,
    73
  vulnerability to lobbying
    25, 43–4, 59, 63, 64, 107,
    123, 138
Grayling, Chris 124
Greece 40–2, 89
Guardian (newspaper) 50, 54

guideline daily amount (GDA)
  43–4
Gulf of Mexico 32, 34, 36–8,
  48, 53, 63, 130, 139

Halliburton 36, 37
Harris Federation 78
Harris, Lord 78
Hartnett, David 119
Hayek, Friedrich von 12–14,
  26, 39, 91–2, 98–9, 142
Hayward, Tony 37
health services
  affordability of 83–4
  consultancies 106
  corporate links 107
  democratic debates 145
  ethics in 1–2, 10, 72, 95
  financial incentives 1–2, 5,
    95
  funding of 148
  Hayekian approach 13–14
  health care as citizenship
    right 124
  improvement in 159
  inability to meet targets 76
  indicator approach 8–9,
    129
  LCP scheme 94–6
  legislative reform 91
  market forces 5, 10–12
  market incentives 71–2
  outsourcing 108–9
  private contracting in 102–3
  queue jumping in 123
  revolving doors
    system 105–7
  sharp practice in 72
  use of assistants 125
Her Majesty's Inspectorate of
  Constabulary (HMIC) 74

Her Majesty's Inspectors of Schools (HMI) 110–12
Her Majesty's Revenue and Customs (HMRC) 109, 117–19, 123
Hewitt, Patricia 106
Hinchingbrooke Hospital, Cambridgeshire 103
Hirschman, A. O. 135, 136
Hoffman La Roche 54
House of Commons Public Accounts Committee 109, 118
HSBC 48, 119
Humboldt, Wilhelm von 140

Independent Police Complaints Commission (IPCC) 80
indicator approach
  abuse of 75–6
  choice of indicators 7–8
  code of ethics for 82
  criticism of 92
  distorting effect 8–9, 75
  and dominance of targets 129
  expansion/simplification 73–4
  finding appropriate indicators of things 92
  gaming of performance indicators 76–80
  government involvement 74
  league tables 80–2, 92–3
  nudge technique 8
  political popularity 71
  political pressures 9–10
  problems caused by 11–12
  proxy indicators 74
  within a market 93

information asymmetries 138, 147, 149, 153, 154, 155, 158
Inland Revenue *see* Her Majesty's Revenue and Customs (HMRC)
inspection regimes 110–13, 130, 150–3, 160, 161
International Monetary Fund (IMF) 41

journal publication 78–9
JPMorgan Chase 46

Keogh, Sir Bruce 81–2
knowledge
  arcane 29
  communication of 30
  conflict with other expertise 35–42
  control, distortion, corruption of 3, 26, 44–53, 131–2, 138
  of elites 11
  generation/dissemination of 53–6
  honest/trustworthy 19–24
  and making satisfactory choices 10–14, 85
  market reliance on 3
  need for 17–18
  neoliberalism as enemy of 2, 87–8
  and the private sector 29
  privatization of the public good of 56–62
  problems unresolved by the market 14–18
  professional 4–5, 29, 110–16, 129–30, 147
  and public services 3

rejection of 89–90
and restricted self 26–9
of self 3–4
suppression of 32–5
and wealth/power 24–6
and withholding of
    information 42–4
Koch brothers 53
KPMG 106

Lansley, Andrew 106
Le Grand, Sir Julian 71–2,
    131
legal system 123–4
Leveson Report (2012) 51,
    69
Libor (London InterBank
    Offered Rate) 45–6
Liverpool Care Pathway (LCP)
    94–6
London Borough of Barnet
    119–20, 122–3, 126
London Olympic Games 108

Manzoni, John 107
Marcuse, Herbert 28
market analogue approach 15,
    40, 110, 129, 131
market theory
  benefits 7
  choice through simple
    indicators 6–7
  efficient 15–17
  and honest dealing 23–4
  monopoly power/control 3,
    131–2
  problems of indicator
    approach 7–10, 18
  purchasers as passive 136
  pure market vs
    oligopoly 20–1

as rational choice 3, 130–1
  weakness of 18
markets
  advocates 5–6
  and confusion of
    inadequacy/self-seeking
    bias 11
  and knowledge necessary
    for satisfactory choice
    10–14
  prioritization of financial
    knowledge 3, 130
  and problems of knowledge
    14–18
  and product complexity 15
  and public service behaviour
    3, 129–30
  regulatory intervention
    147
  and reputation 20, 21
  role of neoliberalism 6
  self-centred/amoral
    behaviour 33–4, 132
  speed of decision systems
    88–9
  theory of 6–10
  and trust 6, 17, 18–24, 153
  wealth/power 24–6
mass media
  attacks on individuals 50–1
  bias/distortion in 49–53
  coverage of league tables
    80–2
  and individual freedom of
    expression 52–3
  integrity of information 49
  journalistic pressures 51
  and market honesty 51–2
  phone hacking 50
  political/corporate interests
    53

mass media (cont.)
  professional/ethical
    standards subordinated to
    profit maximization 50–1,
    69, 69–70, 132
  state-regulated 141
  undermining of professional
    reputations 156
Merck 54
Milburn, Alan 106
Mill, John Stuart 52
Ministry of Defence 105
Mirowski, P. 12, 26
Monsanto Chemicals 60
Mont Pèlerin Society 12, 26,
  27
Moody's 20
Murdoch, Rupert 51, 53, 141

National Audit Office 109
National Border Agency 103
National Health Service
  (NHS) 1, 54, 82, 91, 95,
  102–3, 105–6, 108–9
National Institutes of Health
  55
National Nuclear Laboratory
  103
National Oceanic Atmospheric
  Administration 37–8
Navdanya 61
Neoliberal Thought Collective
  12–13, 26
neoliberalism
  attack on knowledge 85–8
  challenges to 83–5
  claims concerning 3–4,
    128–32
  corporate 3, 42–3
  and employees' rights 139
  as enemy of knowledge 2–3

  and facilitation of
    competition 62
  and the individual 27–9
  and introduction of market
    analogues 15, 40, 110,
    129, 131
  and knowledge of market
    process itself 10–14
  and making choices 135
  and market as perfect store
    of knowledge 26–7
  motivation through
    self-interest 10
  people as objects 135–6
  privatization/contracting out
    131
  professionals in public
    services 99–100, 131
  professionals as satisfactory
    153
  and regulation of
    externalities 139
  undermining of professional
    knowledge 113
Neuberger, Lady 95
new public management
  (NPM)
  acceptance of 94–6
  assessment of performance
    68, 70, 71
  and citizens/customers
    139
  and concentration of power
    68
  decentralization/closeness to
    consumers 68
  erosion of barriers 112
  ethics in 88, 99
  and management by
    objectives 67, 68
  neoliberal principles 91–2

private finance initiatives
159
in public services 67–71,
82, 88, 90
public/private contact 152
revolving doors system 107
New York Times (newspaper)
37, 124
News Corp 51, 53, 141
News of the World
(newspaper) 50, 51, 52,
141
NHS England 106
NHS for Sale (2015) 103
Nissen, Steven 55
No Patent on Seeds 61
Nokia 104
Nordic industrial relations 62
Nuclear and Industrial Safety
Agency 38
nudge technique 8, 28, 73, 87,
117, 124–5
Nuffield Trust 76

Obama, Barack 8, 37
Office for Standards in
Education, Children's
Services and Skills
(Ofsted) 110–13
Ofqual 78
old people's homes *see* elderly
care
O'Neill, Onora 6, 52, 76,
150–1
Organic Seed Growers and
Trade Association 60
Organisation for Economic
Co-operation and
Development (OECD)
67–8
Osborne, David 67

outsourcing 100, 128, 158
children in care 113–14
contract allocation 106–8
creation of markets 126
new economy of 101–10
old people's homes 114–15
priorities 110
professional knowledge
110–16
public services 100, 101–10,
122–3, 125–6
quality of service 115–16
reduction in skill level 125
revolving door characteristic
105
scandals 108–15
school inspections 110–13
successful initiatives 125

Paterson, Owen 98
Paxil 55
payment protection insurance
(PPI) 47–8, 51
pharmaceuticals industry
54–5
Philip Morris International 56
Piketty, Thomas 84
police 73–4, 80, 108, 129,
145
Policy Exchange 124
Press Complaints Council 50
PricewaterhouseCoopers 106
professionals 10, 127
confident/approachable
156–7
customers as citizens 156
democratic aspects 148–9
feminization of 157
inspection regimes 150–3
knowledge 4–5, 29, 110–16,
129–30, 147, 149

professionals (cont.)
  neoliberal view of 99–100
  and public participation
    153–8
  stereotypes 156
  trust in 149, 151
  and whistle-blowers 156
public knowledge goods
  alphabet 57
  atomic table 57
  monopoly rights 58
  ownership issues 56–62
  patents/intellectual property
    protection 58, 59–62,
    132
  and pirating of recorded
    music, film, entertainment
    58
  and tragedy of the commons
    57
public services
  affordability 83–4
  application of market
    analogues to 15, 131
  assessment of performance
    71–82
  changing priorities of
    85–6
  communication difficulties
    157–8
  consumer choice 6–7, 73
  contract allocation 106–8
  contracting out 29–30
  critique of 116
  and customer choice 73
  customers as objects 116,
    154, 157
  ethics in 72, 92, 95–6
  imposition of market values
    83–8
  inadequacies in 71

incentives for improvement
    67–8
individual/collective interests
    84
and information asymmetry
    155–6
knights/knaves concept
    71–2, 99, 131
monitoring of 68
and neoliberalism 67, 83–8
and new public management
    (NPM) 67–71, 82, 88
nudging activity 73
organizational form 105
priority of speed 88–92
privatization/outsourcing
    project 100, 101–10,
    125–6, 131, 136
professionalism/ethics in 68,
    70, 72
and the profit motive 72–3
real market situation 10–12
reform of 154
rich/poor distinction 136
role/power of professional
    service provider 29
Ryanair model 119–22
setting targets/producing
    scores 6, 7–10, 67, 71–82
speed of decision system
    90–2
strong customer approach
    155
suspicions concerning
    professionals in 99
user as customer 116–19

Qatari Investors Group 114

rail travel 116–17
Rand Corporation 76

ratings agencies 19–21, 40, 153
rational choice 3, 23–4, 130–1
Reagan, Ronald 97
Reid, Lord 105
research, sponsorship of 53–6
revolving doors system 105–7
Rice-Tec 61–2
Rochdale 114
Rotherham police 74
Royal Bank of Scotland (RBS) 46, 114
Ryanair model 126
  co-pilots as stewards 121, 125
  in London Borough of Barnet 119–20, 122
  restraint on choice 120–1
  role of customers 122
  stripped-down approach 121
  success of 120

SABMiller 107
Schekman, Randy 79
Seaton, Jean 141
Serco 101, 103–4, 108–10, 112
Seroxat 54
Sewell, Dennis 97–8, 100
sexual crime 73–4, 131
shopping centres/local shops 120–1
The Simpsons (cartoon) 141
Sky News 141
Smith, Adam 23–4
Social Enterprise Report (2012) 101, 103–4

Social Enterprise UK 101, 109, 114
social enterprises 101
Southern Cross 114–15, 130
Southern Homes 114
Spectator (magazine) 98
Spires Academy, Oxfordshire 77
Spottiswoode, Claire 105
Spottiswoode inquiry (2000) 73
Staffordshire hospitals 81–2, 100
Standard Chartered 48
Standard and Poor's 20
Steven, Simon 105–6, 108
stock market trading 15–17
student-customer 7–8, 26, 85–8, 117
Sunstein, C. R. 8
Sweden 102, 103

Talisman (oil fracking company) 107
Tamiflu 54
taxpayer-customer 117–19
TEPCO (Tokyo Electric Power Company) 33, 36, 38
Tesco 44
Texas 75–6, 77
Texas City 107, 130
Thaler, R. H. 8
Thatcher, Margaret 12, 89
'too big to fail' concept 104, 109, 127, 131, 132, 136
Trades Union Congress (TUC) 102
Tribal 112
Troika 41–2
Tuck, Penelope 117, 118
Tucker, Paul 46

UBS 46
UK Financial Conduct
    Authority 46
UK Financial Services
    Authority (FSA) 45,
    47
UK Food Standards Agency
    43, 44
Unite (trade union) 107
United Health 105–6
United Nations 109
university research 55–6,
    78–80
    see also education
University of Zurich 56
US Chemical Safety and
    Hazard Investigation
    Board (USCSHIB) 36
US Food and Drug
    Administration (FDA)
    55
US Minerals Mining Service
    38

US Office of Information and
    Regulatory Affairs 8
US Supreme Court 60

vehicle emissions 17–18
Vioxx 54, 55

Warwick Mansell 77–8
Welch, Stephen 145–6
West Sussex Country Council
    114–15
Which? 122
The Wire (TV series) 66–7
World Economic Forum
    (Davos) 26
World Health Organization
    (WHO) 54
World Trade Organization
    (WTO) 62

Yarl's Wood, Bedfordshire 109

Zimmer, Daniel 147